THE
PALEO
JOURNEY

THE
PALEO
JOURNEY

RECIPES FOR WEIGHT LOSS, ALLERGIES, AND SUPERIOR HEALTH—THE NATURAL WAY

SIMONE MCGRATH

Skyhorse Publishing

Skyhorse Publishing books may be purchased in bulk at special discounts for sales promotion, corporate gifts, fund-raising, or educational purposes. Special editions can also be created to specifications. For details, contact the Special Sales Department, Skyhorse Publishing, 307 West 36th Street, 11th Floor, New York, NY 10018 or info@skyhorsepublishing.com.

Skyhorse® and Skyhorse Publishing® are registered trademarks of Skyhorse Publishing, Inc.®, a Delaware corporation.

Visit our website at www.skyhorsepublishing.com.

10 9 8 7 6 5 4 3 2 1

Library of Congress Cataloging-in-Publication Data

Names: McGrath, Simone.
Title: The Paleo journey : recipes for weight loss, allergies, and superior
   health-the natural way / Simone McGrath.
Description: New York, NY : Skyhorse Publishing, [2016]
Identifiers: LCCN 2015050123 (print) | LCCN 2016005873 (ebook) | ISBN
   9781510705876 (hardback) | ISBN 9781510705883 (ebook) | ISBN 9781510705883
   Subjects: LCSH: High-protein diet—Recipes. | Reducing diets—Recipes. |
   Prehistoric peoples—Nutrition. | Cooking (Natural foods) | BISAC: COOKING
   / Health & Healing / Weight Control. | COOKING / Specific Ingredients /
   Natural Foods. | COOKING / Health & Healing / Allergy. | COOKING / History.
Classification: LCC RM237.86 .M37774 2016 (print) | LCC RM237.86 (ebook) |
   DDC 641.5/638—dc23
LC record available at http://lccn.loc.gov/2015050123

Cover design by Jane Sheppard
Cover photo photographs: iStock Photo

Print ISBN: 978-1-5107-0587-6
Ebook ISBN:978-1-5107-0588-3

Printed in China

The information given here is designed to help you make informed decisions about your health. It is not intended to replace the advice of a qualified health professional. If you have a condition that requires care, please seek treatment with your health-care provider.

CONTENTS

INTRODUCTION
MY STORY

I was sick and tired of being sick and tired—literally!

For almost 40 years I suffered. And then I found Paleo—it changed my life. That was the day my Paleo journey started, and I have never looked back!

I was a very sickly baby. I suffered from diarrhea and bad colic, and I cried a lot from the tummy pains. I was one of those kids who should have just been born and put into a bubble because I was allergic or intolerant to almost everything—dairy, eggs, gluten, peanuts, lamb, dust mites, and cats, to name a few. My mother learned about my life-threatening allergy to peanuts one day when she gave me a bit of peanut butter on toast. My face and throat swelled up almost instantly, and she had to rush me off to the hospital for treatment. As I grew older, I developed mild eczema. I was one of the lucky ones because I outgrew my peanut allergy at around ten years old, but was then diagnosed with asthma at fourteen and also suffered with hay fever, both of which persisted through my teens and into adulthood.

Back then, there was no quick fix like an epi pen to sort out an allergic reaction. Every time something affected me, I had to be rushed off to doctors for treatment. It was very distressing for myself and my family. Allergies and intolerances were not commonplace forty-one years ago like they are today. In fact, I was considered quite a rarity, and my health complaints were all quite serious—I was diagnosed at a 9 (out of 10) for the severity of symptoms I experienced.

When I was diagnosed with all these allergies, there were no specialty health stores that catered to my conditions. You didn't find aisles of gluten- and dairy-free products in the grocery store, and there were no easy, ready-to-eat, quick-fix meals that my mom could buy for me—she had to make everything from scratch. But although it was time-consuming and meant a ton more work for her, she did it for me because it was what I needed (thanks mom!).

I found a wonderful man who accepted that life with me was going to be a little like navigating stormy seas as I battled my allergies and health issues. We got married and had two beautiful children. My daughter was the first born and she too had asthma and hay fever as well as allergies to dust mites, dairy, nuts, and eggs. Just like I did, she suffers from a life-threatening peanut allergy. My son is intolerant to eggs, gluten, and dairy and is allergic to dust mites. As a result, he too had hay fever and eczema.

I tried all the meds prescribed by the doctors, but they all had their own set of side effects, and I eventually stopped. I tried all kinds of natural remedies, most notably the allergy elimination diet and the vegan diet, but I had no success. I was starting to get despondent—was I going to suffer with these things for the rest of my life, and had I doomed my kids to the same fate? The guilt about my kids propelled me to action, and I started intensive research into how to combat these allergies as naturally as possible.

It was late one night, and I couldn't sleep due to my hay fever acting up, so I decided to see if I could find something useful online, and that's when I found Paleo. It was like it was tailored for me specifically, and the deeper I delved the more convinced I became that this was going to be the way forward for my family and me. I began making Paleo recipes almost straight away and was pleased to see that my family seemed to enjoy the new food just as much, if not more. I slowly made the switch to "Paleofying" every meal over a few weeks (more about my family's transition later), and my family is now happy to eat this way every day. They all enjoy the variety of unique recipes on the diet and even help me to prepare them on occasion.

Overall, the change in our health has been nothing short of dynamic! I no longer battle with a long list of health issues, and my husband (who, granted, never suffered allergies in the first place) is thriving mentally and physically from eating this way. My daughter no longer has asthma, and she no longer suffers from any allergies except for nuts. My son's eczema has totally cleared up, and while he is still intolerant to some foods, that is slowly starting to get better too.

The most important thing that has come out of this besides the obvious effects of improved health is that my children now understand first-hand the importance of eating a healthy whole-food diet. That knowledge and the good food habits they have learned and are still learning will be carried through into their adulthood so their children hopefully don't have to suffer as we have—and you cannot put a price on that!

1
PALEO 101
WHAT'S ALL THE FUSS ABOUT?

Modern man is unhealthy—fact!

We are plagued by more disease, illness, allergies, and medical issues than ever before. In fact, it is a fairly safe assumption that the only reason we end up living so long is due to amazing advancements in modern medicine and the resulting pharmaceuticals. In recent years, much research and countless millions have been invested in further discovering how our bodies work, and the results are astoundingly simple.

Science has shown that if we wish to lead long and healthy lives, we need to get in touch with our inner Fred Flintstone to essentially emulate our caveman ancestors. Say what? Yup, that's right, we need to go way back to where it began all those millions of years ago and try to live a lifestyle similar to ancient man.

Well, if the thought of clubbing dinner over the head and dragging it back to your cave doesn't sound appealing, don't worry—you are not alone! I'm not suggesting you start existing on dino-burgers, trade in your new Audi for a pedal-powered car, and stock your wardrobe in the latest of loincloth chic. What I am suggesting is that you take a long, hard look at what you put into your body and make a conscious effort to clean it up—a lot!

Go right now and open your kitchen cupboard and do an honest inventory—how much of what you see do you think truly nourishes your body and adds value to your health? I'll wager not much. We are stuck in an age of convenience, and unfortunately that convenience carries a hefty price tag—our health. Now, I for one am actually not prepared to make that sacrifice anymore. It's time for change and that change is called Paleo!

Now, I'm sure you have probably already heard about the Paleo diet. After all, it's nothing new. It has literally stood the test of time over 2.5 million years. Not many diets can boast these kinds of stats, but that's precisely why Paleo can—it's actually not a diet. Well, not in the traditional sense anyway.

Let me explain. Most diets you go onto for a short period to achieve a specific set of goals like losing weight or detoxing your body, for example, but with Paleo you are wanting to achieve overall health and longevity, and that, my friends, takes commitment. Paleo is not something you do for a few weeks and then start loading your body up with rubbish again. Paleo is long term—it entails a total shift of mindset and redefining the parameters of your relationship with food by rethinking your food choices on a daily basis.

It's time to get healthy, people, and I'm going to show you how!

WHAT IS PALEO?

So here is the lowdown.

Paleo refers to the eating habits of man when he lived during the Paleolithic era 2.5 million years ago when we were hunter-gatherers. Research has been conducted into modern hunter-gatherer societies that exist in the world today and who follow a lifestyle that closely resembles that of our ancient ancestors. The results have shown these civilizations to be largely disease free, which has led to the conclusion that the cavemen must have been pretty healthy. But how? Back then, there were no doctors, there were no medicines, and certainly no hospitals to deal with sickness—so what could account for the health and longevity characteristic of this era? Well, the answer is so simple—food! The food they ate kept them healthy, and so the Paleo diet was born.

Supporters of this lifestyle maintain that it is the food we eat that makes us sick and is largely the cause of what has been dubbed "lifestyle diseases" that are so prevalent in modern society. Things like cancer, diabetes, depression, allergies, infertility, osteoporosis, obesity, Alzheimer's, Parkinson's, and the host of digestive complaints that plague modern man by and large did not exist in the days of early man. This health phenomenon has been researched extensively, and scientists have come to the conclusion that the only plausible reason for the differences in overall health between the cavemen and modern man is diet. So what changed? Why are humans now so disease-ridden?

Again, the answer has been pretty easy to trace, and the blame can be laid at the feet of the agricultural revolution about 10,000 years ago. When the timeline of man was studied, researchers noticed a significant trend that lent huge support to the claims that our diet was slowly killing us. It was noted that cases of these lifestyle diseases began to be reported around 10,000 years ago, too, and as time went on, they began to steadily increase with reported cases skyrocketing in recent years.

What, you may ask, was so special about the agricultural revolution that could account for such dramatic claims? Well, it was around this time that dairy and grains came to be included in our diet as man learned to farm and developed more advanced forms of storage and preservation. As man has gotten "cleverer," there have been huge advancements in food technology, and much of our food is now laden with chemicals, preservatives, colorants, and the like.

However, these huge evolutionary strides that have been made by man have remained limited to industry, societal advancements, and technology. Biologically speaking, we are pretty much exactly the same as we were 2 million years ago and consequently are just simply poorly adapted to process much of what we are eating, namely foods from outside the Paleolithic era. If we want to remain healthy, we need to follow the genetic blueprint laid down for us right in the beginning as we are biologically engineered to eat a diet rich in lean proteins, fruits, vegetables, nuts, and seeds. We need to shun anything with grains, dairy, and refined sugar, for our body is simply not capable of processing it properly. Going back to our evolutionary roots in terms of what we consume is now believed to be an important way to stave off all these modern medical maladies. Going Paleo is the only way to eat for health and longevity as it is the only diet that complements our genetic make-up.

The 10,000 years since the agricultural revolution has seen a radical physical degeneration in the overall state of human health. During the Paleolithic era, man was fit, strong, agile, muscular, and energetic. Today, we are tired, stressed, overweight, and disease-ridden. Homo sapiens evolved from thriving hunter-gatherers who ate real, natural, wholesome, and nutritious foods to farmers who ate processed grains and dairy products to fast-food junkies who exist on processed rubbish. While our lifestyles have certainly undergone a major transformation, our bodies have not. Our baseline genetics have remained fairly constant over the years and have not evolved to be able to tolerate these types of foods in our diets. The Paleo diet thus attempts to rectify the havoc wreaked on our bodies by the inclusion of "impure" foods into our diets and sets us back on a healthier dietary path.

When you think about it, this has huge implications for modern humans. In recent years, fast-food joints have literally sprung up in every far-flung corner of the globe with high-fat, calorie-laden food choices and the inclusion of chemicals, additives, preservatives, and artificial colors and flavors in our foods. This has seen the numbers of health concerns rocket off the charts. Coincidence? I don't think so! Our food is literally poisoning us from the inside out! How many of you have tried to find something "convenient" without it containing dairy and grains—it is almost impossible, and that's not even with me getting on my soapbox about hidden sugars in processed foods. Absolutely everything has one or the other or a combination in it, and absolutely all processed foods are laden with sugar. If you are lucky enough to find something, I would bet my bottom dollar that a quick glance through the ingredients has lists of unpronounceable names or simply letters and numbers as the chemical ingredients. It is unconscionable that we accept this as food. Does it taste nice? Probably. Are the few moments of guilty pleasure worth it? Definitely not!

Usually, when educating people on this ancestral dietary template, I am met with two major resistance movements:

1. "This diet is going to break the bank"
2. "How boring—there are only so many ways to eat fruit and veggies"

I am pleased to dispel both! The beauty of Paleo is that it is completely adaptable—not only to your budget but to your personal taste preferences. Once you have grasped basic Paleo principles, you are limited only by your imagination in the culinary masterpieces you can create. A quick Google search yields thousands of recipes to try. Prosciutto too expensive? Swap it for some bacon. Don't like Brussels sprouts? Leave them out or substitute something else—it is really that simple! There are no more excuses not to embrace good health. Paleo is easy to follow, and if you have a little finesse in the kitchen and let your creative juices flow, the possibilities are literally endless. You can adhere to Paleo principles and still prepare scrumptious three-course meals and the most decadent of desserts without your body paying the price. Guilt-free, yummy meals—sounds like my kind of diet! It's time to take your lives in hand and feed your body from within with good, wholesome food that nourishes not only your body, but your mind and soul, too. So go on, give it a try—you only have good health to gain!

2
THE BLACK, WHITE, AND GREY
WHAT'S ALLOWED, WHAT'S TABOO,
AND WHAT'S UP FOR DEBATE

Right folks, so here is the lowdown—the Paleo diet can basically be summed up in one sentence: "If the cavemen didn't eat it, then neither should you." The premise is simple—if ancient man could hunt it with a spear or gather it from a bush, then you can eat it too. According to this diet, foods that can be eaten raw are considered healthy. Anything processed is taboo—it's really that simple!

So what exactly can you eat? In a nutshell, you need to cut all grains, dairy, refined sugars, alcohol, and any other processed foods out of your diet, and replace them with nutrient-dense, wholesome, "real" foods, like lean proteins, vegetables, fruits, seafood, nuts, seeds, and healthy fats. To best mimic our ancient ancestors, staunch followers of this diet go one step further and only choose organic and free-range food options, but this is not strictly necessary. As with any eating plan, there is contention over the specifics of what should and shouldn't be included, but this gives you the basic framework to work with. It is generally accepted that in the presence of debilitating disease or specific food sensitivities, a stricter stance should be adopted when deciding what foods to say "yes" and "no" to. Once you have mastered the basics, the Paleo world is yours to claim. You will have loads of fun experimenting with new foods and different combinations, and you might be surprised to learn that things you would normally never

have paired together (think bacon and chocolate) might just be a taste extravaganza second to none!

So follow this guide to learn how to stock your house with Paleo essentials. For me, when doing this, I work on the "out of sight, out of mind theory." Purge your house of ALL non-Paleo items, and you are far more likely to succeed on this eating plan. Having said this, people choose to "Paleofy" their lives to varying degrees. For this reason, I have included a section of grey areas to give you the facts so that you can make informed choices about what the best options are for you personally. The ultimate goal of Paleo should be an improvement in the overall state of your health, and therefore you need to be realistic about what you are able to maintain in the long term. Sustainability is key, and you need to approach Paleo sensibly if you want it to last. Deciding to exist on boiled chicken and celery sticks for the rest of your life is going to last about three days—if you're lucky. For me, good, tasty food is non-negotiable. Life is far too short to eat bland food at every meal. The good news is that healthy food does not automatically mean boring, and you can enjoy a wide variety of delicious food at every meal. As an added bonus, you will be far healthier than your friends who are also eating delicious food, but packed full of all the wrong things. Once you start feeling the health benefits of better food choices (and trust me, this won't take long), Paleo will not seem like such a daunting prospect, and all your cravings for the wrong foods will disappear. Give it a try—I can promise you won't be disappointed!

FOODS TO EAT

VEGETABLES

Your mom was right! Veggies are good for you. The more you eat, the better! In order to get the most benefits from vegetables, it is recommended to "eat the rainbow." The greater the variety of type and color veggies you include in your diet, the better the range of vitamins, minerals, and nutrients you will be supplying your body with. Depending on your specific and refined Paleo goals, eating starchy veggies should be kept to a minimum (especially if you are trying to lose a few pounds). This is because when weighed up against their sugar, starch, and carb content, their low nutritional value does not make them the best choice for health. They are not bad for you; there are just better choices out there, like artichokes, asparagus, broccoli, Brussels sprouts, carrots, cabbage, cauliflower, celery, eggplant, kale, lettuce, mushrooms, onions, peppers, parsnips, radishes, spinach, turnips, and zucchini. These are nutritionally dense and will give your body an extra boost without any extra calories. Include them daily, and save the starchy veggies for an occasional treat. Most vegetables and salad ingredients are acceptable on Paleo except for things like white potatoes, green beans, and corn (more about this later), so if you choose to include them, do so sparingly or simply omit them altogether. Sweet potatoes are a versatile, nutritionally dense superfood that serves as an excellent Paleo-friendly replacement to white potatoes.

FRUITS

Fruit is the bomb! Not only are they juicy and tasty, but they are so jammed with vitamins and minerals that they can't possibly be bad for you, and you should include them in your diet on a daily basis. However, despite all the good stuff, they are still high in fructose, and the carbohydrates add up, so you should not consume too many. This is especially important if you are diabetic or trying to lose weight. Fructose is a natural sugar, and while it is certainly better than tucking into a candy bar, it is still sugar. Fructose can be quite heavy on the liver in large quantities and consequently is easily stored as fat. It is best to choose lower carb/calorie options like apples or watermelon for daily consumption and to keep things like bananas, grapes, and pineapple for special occasions.

Fruit, however, as long as it is not eaten in excess, is not inherently bad for you. It is recommended to not have more than five servings of fruit per day, three if you are trying to lose weight. This is a lot of fruit to eat in a day, so if you have a bit of a sweet tooth, you don't have to deprive yourself at all.

Fruit is a delicious treat to combat an attack of the munchies, and you can safely snack on any of the following: apples, apricots, bananas, cantaloupe, cherries, figs, grapes, grapefruit, guava, kiwi, lime, lemon, lychee, mango, melon, nectarines, oranges, papaya, plums, peaches, pomegranate, pears, pineapple, strawberries, tangerine, and watermelon.

It is always best to buy your fruit organic whenever possible.

PROTEIN

On the Paleo diet, you can eat as much meat and eggs as you like. Protein was an important source of nutrition for the cavemen, and it should be for you, too. Most free-range, grass-fed products are allowed on this eating plan, and your guideline should be, "If it used to oink, moo, roar, or bleat, then it's safe for you to eat!" Keeping your meat options organic has a very clear rationale behind it—if over the years humans didn't evolve to be able to process grains, then it is a fairly safe assumption that cows didn't either! Grain-fed meat means that you will be getting the remnants of their diet in your body when you consume them at dinner. Furthermore, commercially farmed meat is loaded full of chemicals, antibiotics, and hormones that help the animals to mature faster, and you most certainly don't want to consume those. Ideally, try to choose lean cuts of meat, and if you can't, simply trim all visible fat off before you cook it.

While you can enjoy all forms of chicken, beef, lamb, turkey, pork, and game meats as often as you like—as well as rare delicacies like quail, duck, ostrich, rabbit, and veal—you should steer clear of highly processed forms of meat like cold cuts, salami, spam, hot dogs, canned meats, and the like. These meats are low-quality nutrition, full of fat, and loaded with MSG and other preservatives and accordingly should be avoided.

Seafood is a highly recommended food—if it swims and has fins and gills, then it's Paleo! Great news for all you seafood junkies out there. Seafood is packed full of nutrition and is a source of omega-3. If you are trying to lose a bit of weight, then fish is definitely the way to go. It can get a little costly, though, so enjoy it as much as your budget will allow!

Eggs are a fantastic source of protein and are a staple in many Paleo recipes. It always amazes me that eggs don't receive more nutritional notoriety, as they truly are amazing. They are one of the few foods that are considered a complete protein because they contain all nine essential amino acids. These are the

building blocks for the human body and provide the energy to keep your active, healthy lifestyle going.

Completely overlooked as a food source in many diets, eggs are surprisingly low in calories when you consider the treasure trove of nutrition they contain. One egg has only 75 calories and 5 grams of fat. It contains 7 grams of high-quality protein as well as a smorgasbord of vitamins, minerals, and carotenoids, which help to keep your body healthy and strong, including iron, folate, selenium, choline, lutein, zeaxanthin, and vitamins A, B12, D, and E.

But what about cholesterol, I hear you shout. One egg contains 213 milligrams of cholesterol—a whopping two thirds of the recommended daily allowance! Well, the latest research indicates that healthy adults can safely enjoy an egg every day without increasing their risk of developing heart disease. In fact, the lutein found in the egg yolk (the part typically thought to be bad for you) might actually offer some protection against the progression of heart disease in its early stages. The American Heart Foundation has conducted research and has downgraded the eggs' villain status to "good guy" once again.

Good news all around, then, especially for us Paleoites! Eggs keep you full for longer, are cost effective, delicious, and so versatile. That coupled with their extensive list of health benefits means it's a no-brainer to up your intake.

NUTS, SEEDS, AND BERRIES

These are a big part of Paleo because they would have been a staple in a hunter-gatherer diet. All nuts and seeds are acceptable as well as the nut butters that are derived from them. Nut butters add a depth of flavor and texture to Paleo baking and produce the most glorious treats that can hold their own against any wheat-based baked goods.

Nuts are highly addictive once you start eating them, but a word of caution—consume them in moderation or you will soon be battling to fasten your jeans! While they are considered "good fats," they are fats nonetheless and if eaten excessively will help you pack on the pounds. Grab a handful of almonds, Brazil nuts, cashews, chestnuts, hazelnuts, macadamia nuts, pistachios, pecans, pine nuts, walnuts, pumpkin seeds, sesame seeds, or sunflower seeds (or a trail mix combo) when you feel hungry, and feel those hunger pangs melt away.

Berries are one of the best things you can consume—like, ever! They are considered to be superfoods and for very good reason. They are packed full of antioxidants, which are basically your fountain of youth—helping keep your young appearance and increasing hair and nail strength. They are a little army of fighters who ward off and repair the damage done to your body by free radicals. Always eat your acai berries, blueberries, blackberries, cranberries, goji berries, gooseberries, raspberries, and strawberries fresh rather than dried. Dried berries contain an extraordinary amount of sugar comparatively, and a lot of their nutritional value gets lost during the drying process.

FATS

The dreaded F-word can strike fear into the hearts of dieters all over the world, but if you know what fats to consume, it isn't nearly so scary. If you are particular about the type of fats you choose, they can be an incredible source of energy for your body. When deciding on what to include, it's natural all the way, baby! Always choose unrefined and minimally processed options, like fresh avocados, avocado oil, coconut oil, coconut milk, flaxseed oil, ghee, macadamia oil, olive oil, red palm oil, and sesame seed oil.

Vegetable oil is a bit of an oxymoron. Its name implies an element of health; after all, veggies are good for you, right? Well, if there was such a thing as broccoli oil or carrot oil maybe, but vegetable oil is actually extremely high in hidden trans fats that oxidize or polymerize when subjected to heat and should be avoided at all costs. Vegetable oil is made when oil is extracted from seeds using solvents like hexane that are highly poisonous during the manufacturing process. Basically, if it can be used to start a car, you don't want it in your body. Period!

DRINKS

Water is the best and healthiest option to drink obviously, but we cannot exist purely on H2O. Most of us enjoy something with a little flavor occasionally, especially on a hot summer day. If you feel the urge for a beverage, an incredibly healthy and tasty option is to make infused water with fresh fruit. Simply chop up your fruit of choice, put it into a jug of water, and allow the flavor to infuse out of the fruit into the water. Served ice cold, this is an incredibly refreshing drink. Another flavorful and revitalizing option is to sip on some chilled coconut water—highly nutritious!

Another option is to drink freshly juiced fruits and vegetables or smoothies made with fruit and coconut milk—these are nutrient-dense options that will elevate your health to superhero status if consumed regularly.

DESSERT

We know that there was no way that the cavemen whipped up a quick chocolate mousse or vanilla cake when they had the neighbors from the cave 2 miles away around for a visit. Well, you would be right, but I'm here to tell you that there is one area where our modern ingenuity has worked in our favor, and that is in Paleo desserts. Yes folks, you can have your cake and eat it, too—100 percent Paleo and guilt-free!

To be a Paleoite, nobody is asking you to emulate the caveman exactly but rather to follow the dietary guidelines laid down in that era. How? you may ask, since sugar is a major component of any dessert. Well, it bears repeating that

there is nothing you have to deprive yourself of on the Paleo diet because you can make your own Paleo-friendly versions of classic desserts. Cakes, cookies, pies, tarts—you can have it all if you simply use the right ingredients. A few simple substitutions and "Bob's your uncle"—in an hour, you could be munching on your favorite dessert. Check out my simple substitutions for sublime desserts.

Wheat-based flours→ nut flours (ground-up nuts) or coconut flour
Butter→ nut butters, ghee
Vegetable oil/canola oil→ olive oil, coconut oil
Milk→ almond milk, coconut milk
Sugar→ raw honey, maple syrup, stevia, coconut palm sugar

Baking powder, baking soda, and vanilla are all Paleo approved and you can even use unsweetened cocoa. And last but certainly not least, you can even enjoy chocolate on the Paleo diet in moderation as long as it is dark chocolate with a 70 percent or higher cocoa content.

If you stock up your pantry with these baking basics, you can satisfy any errant sweet tooth cravings in a jiffy with scrumptious Paleo desserts. Although these desserts are healthier than traditional desserts, it does not mean that you can consume them daily with no adverse effects—just as before, if you binge on desserts you will gain fat. Everything in moderation. Paleo desserts should still be an occasional treat.

FOODS TO AVOID AND WHY

GHASTLY GRAINS

Grains wreak havoc on our systems and should be avoided at all costs and in all forms! Truly, there are no redeeming qualities to grains that could justify their inclusion in our diets, and they need to be banished from your diet—TODAY! There is no grey area, wiggle room, or debate involved—this is one of the two major taboo areas in Paleo. So what exactly is it about grains that gets everybody so hot and bothered? While a total carb embargo is not unusual when dieting, the rationale behind their exclusion is different from traditional diets. In traditional diets, they are excluded for weight-loss reasons, but for Paleo, they are eliminated because they are inflammatory, difficult to digest, and essentially made up of anti-nutrients that do little to nourish your body. In addition, as they are a product of farming, they are heavily processed and, in accordance with baseline Paleo philosophy, processed foods should not be consumed. Grains just simply mess with our systems, and I promise after just a week of being grain-free, you will feel the difference. Grains are one of the big "discoveries" of the agricultural revolution, and while many were excited about the progress since food could now be stored for much longer periods, nobody thought about what the effects would be to our body. Humans are unable to digest or process grains effectively, and because of this they clog up our digestive tracts, cause a host of digestive complaints, and have been linked to a number of different diseases.

Right, so here are the cold, hard facts. Grains contain something called gluten, and gluten gets its name from its glue-like properties. When flour is mixed with water to make dough for bread, biscuits, pastries, and so forth, it forms an intricate sticky web of protein fibers. This web is what enables the dough to rise and bind together when baked. Unfortunately, when we eat it, it retains these glue-like properties in our digestive systems. In severe cases, the body reacts by sending the immune system soldiers out to attack and destroy the foreign invader, treating it almost like it would a bacterial infection. Sometimes in the process, the cells lining the digestive tract get caught in the cross-fire and also become destroyed—NOT GOOD, right? This is known as celiac disease and affects a small percentage of the population.

In the more common cases, the gluten simply results in a host of symptoms that cause mild to severe discomfort depending on your level of intolerance or sensitivity. Things like bloating, flatulence, fatigue, cramps, diarrhea, or constipation and even pain and inflammation in the joints. In some cases, gluten can cause leaky gut syndrome where waste literally leaks out the intestines and into the bloodstream (feeling pretty queasy now?).

Besides all the effects gluten has on the gut, it also affects the brain. Gluten has been shown to slow down thinking and response times as well as impair concentration. It has also been shown to play a role in general cognitive decline—people suffering from certain neurological illnesses like autism, schizophrenia, epilepsy, and Alzheimer's show a marked improvement when gluten is removed from their diet. In addition, grains have been linked to inflammation, fatigue, mood swings, energy dips, and an acidic body state. I'm sure you can all see why it's best to steer a wide berth around grains of all kinds from now on.

Good old modern science has also revealed that grains contain something called phytates, which are what cause all the chaos. Phytates are little devils that prevent the body from absorbing essential nutrients, vitamins and minerals such as zinc, iron, and calcium, and I'm sure I don't need to stress just how bad that could be for you. Imagine what it does to your kids who are still growing and developing. Grains also lack any kind of substantive, specialized, or unique nutritive value that could make their inclusion in our diet necessary. The nutrients that they do contain can be obtained from meat, which has far more beneficial properties and makes it a far better go-to source of nutrition.

Now I hear all you diehard grain fans out there shouting "But what about fiber? Grains are high in fiber!" as you sweat in a state of total panic, contemplating a life without bread, cake, cookies, pasta, and rice. Yes, I will admit that grains are indeed high in fiber, but when weighed up against all the negatives, they are just not the best source of it. Just because something has fiber in it doesn't automatically make it good for you. Fruits and vegetables are far better sources of heart-healthy soluble fiber because, in addition to fiber, they are also loaded with vitamins and minerals, which make them more nutritious and healthy. Fruits and veggies have a host of other health benefits, too.

Grains have also been shown to be an instrumental factor in the development of diabetes because they cause major insulin responses and spikes in your body that are not natural. However, natural sources of carbohydrates provide more sustainable energy that keeps your insulin levels on an even keel, thus reducing horrible food cravings that you get when your sugar levels drop. Grains cause a temporary spike but then drop off dramatically because they are not sustainable, and that, my friends, is when you usually pig out on rubbish!

So folks, bid your farewells to breads, rolls, pasta, noodles, cakes, crackers, pretzels, cookies, bagels, pastries, chips, waffles, pancakes, pizza, doughnuts, muffins, cereals, tortillas, pita bread, and the like. Or rather, I should say bid farewell to the wheat-based versions of these because you can make the most delicious Paleo versions of all of these without any of the awful side effects.

Other grains that should be avoided are amaranth, barley, buckwheat, corn, millet, oats, quinoa, rice, rye, and sorghum.

DISASTROUS DAIRY

As far as dairy products go, consuming them is just unnatural. Period! Mother Nature provides us with the perfect template to follow, but unfortunately humans are the only mammals who choose not to listen. Have you ever seen a tiger baby being suckled by a mother elephant? Or perhaps a zebra baby drinking a giraffe's milk? No? So why do we do it? We are the only mammals who drink the milk of another animal and deem it acceptable practice. Cow's milk is for calves, not humans—end of story! Other mammals in nature feed their own young with milk from their bodies, and that is the way it should be

as laid down by nature. The human body simply does not possess the necessary enzymes to break down cow's milk effectively, and the only reason for this is that we are not supposed to be drinking it. Evolutionarily speaking, dairy products are not actually needed to achieve an optimal state of health.

What has been scientifically proven is that human infants have an enzyme called lactase. Lactase is only produced by the body for the first two years of life, and its function is to break down milk and milk products, specifically a mother's breast milk. Now I realize in our modern, fast-paced life, unfortunate practicalities have to take precedence. The reality is that not all moms stay at home or are capable of nursing their children until their second birthday. As a result, we supplement with formulas that are derived from cow's milk. Now, in the absence of any major milk allergies, your infant will probably be fine on a milk-based formula as they possess lactase to help break it down and process the milk, but what happens after that? Many children go on to continue to consume milk products without any adverse effects, but an ever-increasing number of children are falling victim to dairy intolerance. Why? Because dairy can be found in the most unsuspecting places, and it forms a large part of our modern diet through childhood and into adulthood. It is causing problems because after the age of two, we do not have the enzyme to break it down effectively—our bodies are simply not designed to consume it. We are the only mammals that drink the milk of another species. Nature and evolution cannot be wrong and humans right—some food for thought.

But if some people can consume dairy without adverse effects, why the Paleo blanket ban on all things dairy? For Paleoites, the rationale behind why all dairy products should be eliminated from your diet is straightforward. In addition to the above, they are heavily processed and accordingly should be avoided—this means milk, cheese, butter, yogurt, whey protein powders, cottage cheese, sour cream, whipped cream, and ice cream. The sad reality is that milk might not actually be so bad for us if it wasn't tampered with to such a huge degree. The dairy industry skims all the healthy saturated fat out of the milk. That fat may very well be one of the only redeeming qualities of whole milk that could keep us healthy. In addition, it also undergoes a process called pasteurization, which is tantamount to processing it and renders the enzymes and beneficial bacteria found in it ineffective.

Research has also shown that dairy products cause an inflammatory response in people, acidify the body, and cause spikes in insulin levels—none of that is good for you! And if that's not enough, what about the allergic reactions to the milk protein casein and the intolerances to lactose, two primary components found in dairy? Dairy has also been linked to a number of digestive complaints, most notably leaky gut syndrome, where what you eat flows out of the digestive tract through small holes and enters the bloodstream! Why would you ever want to pollute your body with such "foods??"

Not to mention that the cows from which we get the milk have probably been fed on a grain-based diet rather than a grass-based one. The milk from grain-fed cows is higher in omega-6 fatty acids and lower in omega-3. It is this ratio that triggers inflammatory responses in humans. Furthermore, these cows are pumped full of growth hormones and antibiotics, which means that the by-products of these will be found in their milk. While still not recommended for consumption, grass-fed cows produce a much higher quality milk with higher levels of omega-3 fatty acids and conjugated linoleic acid (CLA), a powerful antioxidant. Interestingly, the healthy components of milk are mostly in the fat, so you can get all the benefits of dairy without the complications of lactose and casein by just consuming butter. Taking it one step further, true Paleoites will rather opt for clarified butter (ghee). Ghee has been melted slowly so that all the milk solids separate and you are left with pure butter fat. This is not only healthy but delicious, too, and highly recommended to include in your diet.

The good news is that there are fantastic Paleo substitutes out there for when you need your fix. Paleo ice cream made with coconut milk is simply superb. Whipped coconut cream is a fantastic replacement for whipped cream, and I have even happened upon a recipe for Paleo cheese! All you are going to be saying goodbye to is all the uncomfortable symptoms and illness associated with consuming products with a cow's milk base. So stock up on your cans of coconut milk, and go buy yourself an ice cream maker so you can be prepared to make delicious ice cream!

SINFUL SUGAR

In my opinion, sugar is one thing that should be avoided like the plague. I treat sugar with the same level of vehemence, caution, and general fear that I would a teaspoon of cyanide! It is the devil—plain and simple! Besides its taste, sugar does not have a single redeeming quality. There is absolutely no nutritional value, and it does not contain a single vitamin or mineral. It has an overwhelming number of calories per gram and is highly addictive—the more you eat, the more you want. Sugar causes dangerous spikes in insulin, and it is precisely these peaks and dips in blood sugar levels that result in the dangerous cravings that derail our otherwise healthy lifestyle. Ideally, we would never start eating it in the first place, but most of us have walked the ill-fated path of sugary sweet temptation, and our inner sugar monster is roaring for more.

I am able to talk about this knowledgeably because I have made all the mistakes and had to learn the things I am telling you here the hard way. I have bribed my kids with sweets, I have eaten too much chocolate, and I

have had two helpings of dessert for dinner. I'm here to tell you, it's time to go cold turkey—right now—today! Just cut it out! Will it be difficult? Without a doubt! Will you regret it? Not for a single second! It will take two weeks of detox and a lot of "Eat me, don't eat me" struggles as you stare down a slice of chocolate cake, but in the end, you will be thankful for breaking what is a terribly destructive dietary habit.

Don't get me wrong, you will still crave sweet things, after all, sugar does have a role to play in our body. It is a vital source of energy, but it all comes down to how we decide to consume it. Stick to natural sources of sweetness like fruits, and if you need to add sugar to anything, use raw honey, stevia, maple syrup, and the like. These are better for you as they do not cause blood sugar levels to spike so dramatically and thus are a more sustained source of energy. The makers of artificial sweeteners (and there are many different brands) would have you believe that these are healthier options, but it is right there in the name *"artificial"*—they are jammed full of chemicals and will damage your body with extended use. Avoid them at all costs.

One of the biggest dangers of processed foods is the amount of hidden sugars they contain. Things you would never expect to contain sugar will leave you gasping at the volume that it contains. Things like granola, which for all intents and purposes is a healthy cereal, contains an enormous 5 teaspoons of added sugar per cup! One-quarter cup of bottled sauce contains 4 teaspoons of added sugar. Scour the internet, and you will find hundreds of equally frightening examples of the hidden sugar that lurks in the most unsuspecting places. This essentially means that even without meaning to, we are probably consuming far more sugar every day than we are even aware of. The only way to control this is to make sure you stay far away from the aisles of processed foods in the grocery store!

OTHER TABOO FOODS

*NOTE!—Peanuts are NOT nuts! Yes, yes, I know it is right there in their name, but they are technically considered to be legumes, and legumes are not Paleo. That means no peanut butter either. Beans are also a big no-no on the Paleo diet, as are all soy-based products like tofu, miso, soy sauce, and bean curd. Say goodbye to broad beans, black beans, kidney beans, fava beans, garbanzo beans, lima beans, mung beans, pinto beans, red beans, white beans, and soy beans. Any other kind of beans, including green beans, peas, black-eyed peas, chickpeas, snow peas, and sugar snap peas are also banned, as are all lentils.

All store-bought fruit juices are taboo—too much sugar and too many preservatives.

Soda is packed FULL of sugar and high fructose corn syrup and is another definite no-no. Get rid of all existing cans and make an oath now to never ever buy more. Soda is one of the worst things you can put into your body—it rots your teeth and rots your gut (pop a piece of steak into a glass of cola if you don't believe me!).

Vegetable oils are high in omega-6 fatty acids and should be avoided.

Yes, I know this all seems very drastic (and it's all the best stuff, right?). I promise you, anything you previously enjoyed eating can be "paleofied." You do not have to go without anything on the Paleo diet other than the nasty side effects of the banned foods! There are Paleo replicas of ice cream, pasta, cookies, cakes, and all of the other "taboo" foods. They are just as easy to make and just as tasty, but you will be healthier for it.

GREY AREAS

ALCOHOL

This is one of the major minefield areas of Paleo—it's Friday night and you want to go out. Everybody will be unwinding with a few drinks, and you are torn between going home and joining them. I'm not going to sugar-coat it—alcohol is not and never will be Paleo. Our caveman ancestors didn't all gather at the end of a long week's hunting and lament their woes over a gin and tonic. HOWEVER, as long as you are not propping the bar up every Friday night, the occasional drink should not do any lasting damage. Our reality 2.5 million years later is that we have become incredibly social creatures, and much of that socializing happens around food and drink. So how do we go about merging the two successfully? Well, fortunately there are options, people! Should you wish to indulge, there are options out there for us Paleoites that are considered "safer." So, for those more adventurous souls out there, did you know that tequila comes from the agave plant so is considered to be acceptable by the more left-wing, liberal Paleoites? Even potato vodka and rum are deemed as okay. This is great news for those who enjoy a social drink. In general, the rules for drinking on the paleo diet are as follows: stick to spirits and mix only with freshly squeezed fruit juice. Avoid soda mixes or any other artificial juices that contain tons of sugar. Keep it simple! Also on the no-no list are beers, ciders, and coolers, as their cup spilleth over with undesirable ingredients. However, if you are really not comfortable with breaking your Paleo

ways, then don't feel pressured—offer to be the designated driver every week to curry favor with your mates and keep the good-natured teasing to a minimum while you sip on one of the many delicious virgin mocktails on offer in most establishments. If you don't want to drink—don't! It's that simple.

TEA AND COFFEE

Now, I know you were probably hoping that I wouldn't mention it, but it has to be discussed—what about your morning cup of tea/coffee (and the mid-morning one, lunch-time one, afternoon one, and bedtime one—am I right?). While I'm sure I don't have to tell you that it's far better to start your day off with some lemon-infused water, I concede that some of us just cannot function without a nice "cuppa" to kick-start our day. If you are one of those people who needs your tea/coffee fix, there are steps to take to make it as Paleo as possible. For tea drinkers, organic and herbal options are obviously best, but you can have the odd standard tea as long as it is in moderation. If you must have standard tea—please do not have it with 4 teaspoons of refined sugar and half a cup of milk! Drink it plain or with a little raw honey or lemon to flavor it. The new flavor might take a bit of getting used to, but your body will thank you for keeping it purged of dairy and refined sugar. For the coffee lovers out there, you can have freshly brewed coffee in moderation, but again no sugar or milk, please!

WHITE POTATOES

If you think about it, when the men went out to hunt the meat, the women went off to gather what would go with the meat, and probably a large proportion of what they gathered would be tubers. Now while white potatoes only came along many years later, as I have said before, we are not looking to only eat foods that were available during the Paleolithic era—we are looking to base our current diets on evolutionary principles, and from that perspective, potatoes would then be acceptable fare. White potatoes, as a Paleo debate, have been around since the dawn of the diet, and they have been the center of much controversy. Many maintain that they are starchy vegetables full of anti-nutrients that do precious little for you other than expand your waistline. Others tout their high glycemic index as a reason to avoid them as they cause dangerous spikes and dips in blood sugar levels. Some people shun potatoes because they are part of the nightshade family. But so are tomatoes, bell peppers, and eggplant, and we don't see everyone getting their knickers in a twist about those. Nightshades are sometimes believed to be bad for you because they contain something called glycoalkaloids, which are believed to trigger leaky gut syndrome in people that are intolerant to them. However, that accounts for such a small percentage of people that to justify their exclusion based solely on that seems a bit extreme. What is interesting to note is that the majority of glycoalkaloids are in the potato skin, so peeling them before cooking would also eliminate the problem. Still others say that the potato should be avoided because it is typically consumed in highly processed forms—think French fries and potato chips. In line with this, I think it is not so much the potato that is the problem but rather the way we choose to eat them. Generally, plain old boiled potatoes are not very appetizing. It's only when we drench them in creamy sauces, butter, and cheese that they become the drool-worthy food that many of us crave. Naturally, on Paleo you cannot eat them covered in dairy, and if you are going to make French fries, you need to fry them in ghee or coconut oil, not the traditional option of vegetable oil. There are those who say that the occasional white potato in a stew or baked in the oven and eaten as is will not do you any harm—so it would appear that it's all in the way you choose to serve them.

GOAT PRODUCTS

Some have suggested that goat's milk might be a good substitute for cow's milk because it has less casein and lactose, has more fat, causes fewer digestive upsets, and is the closest in structure and nutritional value to human breast milk. But this is another grey area up for debate and should be consumed cautiously until you are sure it is not doing your body harm. Goat products are another matter of personal choice and how tolerable you find them.

HERBS, SPICES, AND CONDIMENTS

These are without a doubt the key to remaining sane on the Paleo diet and sticking with it! They enable you to jazz up anything in the most creative and appetizing ways and allow you to turn something plain and boring into a culinary

masterpiece. (And let's face it, who can live without ketchup??) The trick here is to stick to low-sodium condiments and the freshest of herbs. Seasoned Paleoites often have their own little herb gardens where they just pick the produce fresh as they need it.

Condiments are an incredibly grey area. Most often, store-bought sauces, jams, marmalades, mustards, and ketchups all contain hidden ingredients. They are gluten-stuffed and packed full of all kinds of preservatives. When shopping for these items, you need to read and examine food labels very closely and always shop with the motto *"if in doubt, leave it out."* In general, though, anything that can sit on a supermarket shelf for extended periods of time without refrigeration should be avoided, as they are likely jammed full of preservatives to keep them from going bad. Don't fall into the trap of being tempted by labels promising "low-fat," "gluten-free," or "sugar-free," as these too could be loaded with artificial colors, artificial flavors, preservatives, additives, and MSG. When on Paleo, always try to get the freshest produce, and in most instances that means making your own. That way, you are 100 percent sure of what you are putting into your body.

Fortunately, if there is something you simply cannot do without, there are many recipes online to make your own. You can make Paleo-friendly versions of anything from ketchup to mayonnaise to BBQ sauce to mustard and even your own Worcestershire sauce. Gravies can be made with organic stock and thickened with arrowroot powder and taste just as hearty as the traditional versions. It is also a good idea to do a bit of research and educate yourself on the substitutions you can make; for example, soy sauce is banned, but an excellent substitute is coconut aminos, which are completely Paleo-safe. Balsamic is for me an absolute essential in any Paleo kitchen—it enhances everything from meat to salad to veggies. Garlic and chilies add depth and flavor to almost all dishes, and with a little practice, you will become a pro at combining herbs and spices. I highly recommend finding your local Indian spice market. Here you will be amazed at the range of fresh spices you can find at very reasonable prices. You can create totally unique flavors every night of the week!

3
THE BENEFITS OF FOLLOWING PALEO

The Paleo Diet is slowly taking over the world with more and more people converting to this way of eating. This is not some revolutionary "flash in the pan" diet of the moment with miracle promises of well-being. Rather, Paleo is the dietary blueprint for health laid down by our genetics.

The widespread popularity of this way of life can be attributed to the proof literally being in the proverbial pudding. The health benefits that are being observed and recorded, not only by followers of this eating plan, but by scientists, are numerous.

Adopting a cleaner, purer, and more natural diet goes a long way in keeping disease and sickness at bay. In addition, eating Paleo will help keep your weight in check, give you more energy, increase your muscle mass, and give your skin a healthy and radiant glow. Not only has this diet stood the test of time over millions of years, but it has held its own under modern scientific scrutiny. There is a host of scientific evidence to back up the claims that the Paleo diet is the best way for us to eat if we want our body to function optimally and to keep us looking and feeling our best. While everyone gets involved in Paleo for their own reasons and will experience individualized results depending on their own body's reaction to the diet, everyone who follows this eating plan agrees that when you eat this way, you feel pretty darn awesome!

Let's take a closer look at some of the many benefits you can expect to enjoy on the Paleo diet. (This is the part where I convince you to give this diet a real go!)

1. Sustained weight loss—if there was ever something to sell you on the diet, being lean, trimmed, and toned is it. The Paleo way of eating and embarking on a more active lifestyle means that you will lose weight, get fitter, and build muscle without even really trying. This is largely due to

improved metabolic processes that aid in burning off all that stored body fat.

2. No more blaming the dog for your gas! When you eat this way, you are naturally upping your fiber and water intake and reducing your sodium, which goes a long way toward improving digestion and reducing uncomfortable bloat that is typically associated with a diet high in processed foods.

3. No more hunger means no more cheating. This diet balances your blood glucose levels naturally. When your blood sugar levels drop, you get those awful hunger pangs that are usually accompanied by cravings for all the wrong foods and the horrid side effects of being irritable, suffering from fatigue, and feeling dizzy. This is known as hyperglycemia and can be accompanied by some crazy mood swings and energy drops. Eating Paleo keeps you comfortably satiated, and the energy released from your food is done in a slow, even manner throughout the day rather than in short bursts that leave you feeling drained afterwards. Your blood sugar levels remain stable, and thankfully so do your moods!

4. Your body gets all the right types of fats which are essential to maintain healthy arteries, proper brain function, and glowing skin, and also play a role in reducing inflammation.

5. You sleep better. Not only do you fall asleep more easily, but you have better quality sleep when eating Paleo because you are cutting out all the additives and chemicals that override the production of serotonin. Serotonin is the chemical that is released signaling that it is time to sleep. And because you are sleeping better, you will wake up far more energized and ready to tackle the day.

6. You'll have more energy. Your body is properly fueled to function through the day without that dreadful afternoon slump. There is no calorie counting on Paleo. You eat when you are hungry, and you eat until you are full—no risk of running out of steam halfway through the day.

7. Clear skin and healthy hair—all those extra vitamins and minerals will make you glow!

8. A healthy brain and mental clarity—you can think properly because your body and brain are purged of all the chemicals and toxins that can clog them up.

9. Improvement in the symptoms of depression and anxiety.

10. Your food is full of antioxidants and phytonutrients, which means less risk of cancer, diabetes, heart disease, and all the other terrible lifestyle diseases that plague society.

11. Improved immune system function means less illness and a general overall sense of health and well-being. It is a good idea to drink bone broth to boost the immune system even further. Broth is an excellent source of vitamins and minerals like calcium, magnesium, and phosphorus. It has been known to improve digestion, allergies, and brain health and contribute to strong bones and teeth, and healthy joints, skin, hair, and

nails. All around, you cannot go wrong drinking such a nutrient-dense liquid on a regular basis, and it's so easy and inexpensive to make. This is the recipe I make for my family. I always make sure there is some in the fridge (it holds for seven days), and our favorite way to drink it is as a warm morning drink with a teaspoon of ghee and a tiny pinch of salt. Totally delightful!

BODY BOOSTING BONE BROTH

INGREDIENTS

3 pounds bones (beef, chicken, or lamb)

2 chicken feet (optional, but provides extra gelatin, so highly recommended)

1 onion, peeled and chopped

2 carrots, peeled and chopped

2 stalks of celery, chopped

1 bunch parsley, chopped

2 garlic cloves, crushed

2 tablespoons apple cider vinegar

1 teaspoon peppercorns, crushed

1 bay leaf

DIRECTIONS

1. Place the bones into a large stock pot and pour enough water over them to cover the bones completely, then add the vinegar and allow it to sit for an hour. The acid from the vinegar makes the nutrients from the bones more available.
2. Add everything else to the pot except the parsley and garlic, then bring the pot to a vigorous boil. Once boiling, reduce to a low simmer and leave for 8 hours, covered, adding extra water if necessary.
3. As the broth simmers, skim any scum off the top and discard it.
4. Add the parsley and garlic for the final hour of cooking.
5. Remove from the heat and allow to cool, then strain all the pieces using a fine mesh strainer.
6. Store in the fridge or freeze for later use.

12. You may have fewer allergies and allergic symptoms.
13. Paleo diet is anti-inflammatory, and people have reported a reduction in the pain that generally accompanies inflammatory conditions.
14. You may see improvements in respiratory complaints like asthma.
15. Better gut health—this diet helps you to detox your body and purge it from the buildup of waste from previous bad eating habits. Your gut flora are naturally healthier, so you experience fewer digestive complaints, and accordingly you are better able to absorb the nutrition from your food. One of the best ways to restore your gut flora naturally is by eating fermented foods—far healthier than taking powdered probiotics. The above recipe for bone broth is also incredibly healing for the gut because of all the gelatin it contains.

As fermented foods form a big part of my life, I want to educate you on the amazing benefits of eating fermented foods. Basically, fermented foods have been through a process called lacto-fermentation. This means that lactic acid is created from natural bacteria feeding on the sugar and starch in the food. Not only does this preserve the food, but it also creates beneficial enzymes, various strains of probiotics, omega-3 fatty acids, and B vitamins. Naturally allowing foods to ferment not only preserves the nutrients in our food, but helps to break the food down to a more digestible form, which in turn leads to improved and easier digestion. Probiotics are very important in the gut because they have been shown to prevent the development of disease, they improve overall bowel health, they help to remove toxins from the body, and they boost immunity.

Note: When first trying fermented foods, always start slowly with a teaspoon and build up gradually to avoid any unwanted detox effects.

I'm going to share with you a few of my favorite fermented food recipes so you, too, can enjoy the benefits of eating this way.

SAUERKRAUT

INGREDIENTS:

2 heads of red cabbage

2 heads of green cabbage

¼ cup salt

DIRECTIONS:

1. Place the cabbage into a sterilized jar and pound it down using a wooden spoon until the juices start to release the liquid. Sprinkle the salt over the cabbage as you go. The salt will draw the water out of the vegetables. If the extracted water does not cover the vegetables when you are done, make a brine out of 2 tablespoons of salt mixed into 4 cups of water and add it to the jars. Take care to leave about an inch at the top of the jars to allow for the vegetables to expand as they ferment.

2. Place the jars into a warm spot in your kitchen, and be sure to weight the lid down and cover the jar with a cloth to keep any flies and bugs away.
3. Allow to ferment for 7–10 days, checking on it periodically to ensure that the vegetables are still covered in brine.
4. You will have to taste it to test if it's ready. When you are happy with the taste, place it into the fridge and enjoy as needed.

SALSA

(Yields 10–12 cups)

INGREDIENTS:

12 cups tomatoes, freshly chopped

2 cups chilies, seeds removed and chopped

¼ cup dried oregano

¼ cup salt

2 onions, chopped

10 garlic cloves, chopped

DIRECTIONS:

1. Mix all the ingredients together in a bowl.
2. Add the mixture to sterilized jars little by little, pounding it down as you go and adding a little salt. Take care to leave an inch at the top of the jars to allow for expansion as they ferment.
3. Place the jars into a warm spot in your kitchen, and be sure to weight the lid down and cover the jar with a cloth to keep any flies or bugs away.
4. Allow to ferment for 3–5 days, checking on it periodically to ensure that the vegetables are still covered in brine and to remove any mold that may have developed.
5. You will have to taste it to test if it's ready. When you are happy with the taste, place it into the fridge and enjoy as needed.

PICKLES

INGREDIENTS:

16 cups pickling cucumbers

16 garlic cloves, peeled and left whole

2 bunches dill

¼ cup salt mixed with 8 cups water

6 tablespoons salt

1 tablespoon peppercorns

1 tablespoon mustard seeds

1 tablespoon cloves

3 bay leaves

DIRECTIONS:

1. Soak the cucumbers for a few hours and then scrub them well. This is to prevent any mold from forming during the fermentation process.
2. Place the cucumbers into a sterilized jar and sprinkle them with salt as you go, then add the rest of the ingredients.
3. Fill the jar with the brine mixture, then place the jars into a warm spot in your kitchen, and be sure to weight the lid down and cover the jar with a cloth to keep any flies or bugs away.
4. Allow to ferment for 5–10 days, checking on it periodically to ensure that the vegetables are still covered in brine.
5. You will have to taste it to test if it's ready. When you are happy with the taste, place it into the fridge and enjoy as needed.

KIMCHI

INGREDIENTS:

2 heads of cabbage

6 carrots, peeled and sliced

2 radishes, peeled and sliced

1 bunch spring onions, sliced

1¼ cups salt

½ cup chili paste

¼ cup fish sauce

16 garlic cloves, chopped

2 tablespoons freshly grated ginger

DIRECTIONS:

1. Soak the cabbage leaves overnight in a mixture of 1 cup of salt and 1 gallon of water.
2. Discard the brine and combine the cabbage with the rest of the ingredients.
3. Place the mixture into a sterilized jar and pound it down to release the liquid. If the liquid doesn't cover the veggies, make a brine of 4 cups of water mixed with 2 tablespoons of salt and cover the veggies properly.
4. Place the jars into a warm spot in your kitchen, and be sure to weight the lid down and cover the jar with a cloth to keep any flies or bugs away.
5. Allow to ferment for 5–7 days, checking on it periodically to ensure that the vegetables are still covered in brine and to remove any mold that may have developed.
6. You will have to taste it to test if it's ready. When you are happy with the taste, place it into the fridge and enjoy as needed.

At the end of the day, I'm just a mom on a mission—a mission to help you provide your family with a healthy lifestyle. Why would you simply want to survive when you can thrive? And thrive you will on Paleo. After looking at the above list of health benefits, you simply cannot contest that Paleo is the best diet out there for your health. It has been proven that the average new Paleoite starts to feel an improvement in energy levels after the first seven days. After a few weeks, things like weight loss start to become visible, and a greater sense of wellness is reported after following Paleo for more than a month. Give it a go—a real go—for one month, and see for yourself. If you choose not to follow it, all you will have lost is thirty days, but if, like the rest of us, you have an awakening, that one month will have set the tone for the rest of your life (not to mention that it sounds pretty cool to tell your friends, "I went Paleo!").

4
PALEO LIFESTYLE FACTORS

EXERCISING

There is nothing more "Paleo" than exercise! Cast your mind back to the days where it all began. Cavemen were fit, strong, and had enough stamina to last for days. Their feet were the only mode of transport, so whether hunting, gathering, relocating, or simply visiting the neighboring tribe, they were constantly on the move. They used to run for days, tracking prey over many miles, then found the strength to bring it down with their weapons, whether this was from afar with arrows or in closer combat with sharpened stones made into primitive knives—either way, they had to be pretty strong to do it. Then they had to haul that prey all the way back to their caves over endless miles to deliver it for cooking. Now, while I'm certainly not suggesting they weren't tired afterwards, they had enough energy to pull it off, over and over, probably every couple of days. In many cases, modern men and women can barely walk up a flight of stairs without collapsing in a heap and fighting for breath.

The essence of modern man is overweight and unfit, whereas ancient man was fit, toned, lean, and muscular. When you think about what the cavemen ate, it really puts things into perspective. Carbs are generally and erroneously believed to be the source of energy that our body needs and most especially when we are exercising. But this is a double-edged sword—our body does need carbs to function, but it goes back to the source of carbs. Carbs are also not needed exclusively—our body needs other things, too, to support an active lifestyle. The Paleo diet is exactly what the human body needs to perform at its peak. It promotes protein as the most important component, which is essential to build a healthy body and muscles. Carbs for energy come from far more natural sources and consequently provide a sustainable source of energy instead of the insulin spikes and dips caused by eating all the "bad carbs." Then you have nuts, seeds, berries, fruits, and veggies, which are all so full of nutrition that you are revitalizing your body from within.

While we no longer have to run for miles just to get dinner anymore, exercise is an essential component to good health. It gets the heart rate up, the blood pumping, and you just can't beat the rush of endorphins you get after a grueling workout. Exercise, therefore, not only has a physical component but a psychological one, too, and is hugely beneficial to overall good health. So what kinds of things should you do to get the most benefit from exercise?

True to form, Paleo exercise is built on the same principles as the actual diet and that is to simply do what your body was designed to do. It moves away from traditionally accepted forms of exercise like gym machines and the like and rather looks at ways to incorporate movement into your life—remember the cavemen were constantly moving with their nomadic hunter-gatherer lifestyle. It should aim at upping the level of activity in daily life rather than waking up an hour early and working out in the gym like a crazy person, then spending the rest of the day sedentary in a chair. Paleo exercise should complement and enhance your diet by strengthening your body and equipping it to rise to the physical challenges of the world. Now granted, in general, the human race is no longer particularly active anymore. Cars take us where we need to go, and many of us are stuck behind a desk all day. Paleo exercise does not look to emulate the cavemen exactly but to adapt the basic principles and make them workable in a modern world. The fact is, we have evolved, and we are privy to a large amount of modern conveniences that we need to make work for us in the best way possible so as to optimize our health.

With Paleo, there are untold benefits to eating the way we were designed to eat, so it should not be a surprise that you can enjoy similar benefits by moving the way your bodies were built to move. Regular exercise improves your longevity by staving off diabetes, osteoporosis, and stroke, and keeps your heart healthy, too. Exercise keeps your muscles and body strong and keeps your immune system functioning at its peak. Your quality of life will improve dramatically because your exercise regime will help to reduce stress and relieve the symptoms of depression. You will sleep better, have improved memory, more energy, and a fit and toned body!

There is no one right or wrong way to approach fitness while you are on Paleo, but you should try to follow the principles of natural movement over other kinds. This will allow your body to reap the maximum benefits of physical activity and avoid the negative effects like injury, muscle spasm, muscle strain, and pain associated with forcing your body to move in ways that are not natural. To keep in line with the natural approach to Paleo, try to find activities that you can do outdoors, like hiking, walking, or jogging, as opposed to machine-based workouts in the gym. If you have to go to the gym for whatever reason, try to stick to free weights and more natural cardio machines like the treadmill that mimic natural movements better than elliptical trainers and the like. Free weights engage your stabilizer muscles better than the machines do and provide a better-rounded workout by working more muscle groups with each exercise. Go for higher weights at lower reps to increase your strength and muscle mass. While gym machines seem to fit in well with our fast-paced modern world, and they do *seem* to do the job adequately, the reality is that they only work a small range of muscles and in isolated, unnatural ways. Paleo exercise seeks to reconnect you with your body's natural activity patterns, so when you spend an hour moving in a mechanical way and then go to work and sit at a desk all day, you end up in a fundamentally disconnected state. Rather, exercise should focus on mimicking movements you might need to do outside the context of the gym. Great options to challenge your natural movement skills require you to get in touch with your inner child—find a playground with some monkey bars and have a go, or climb a tree—I can guarantee you will find muscles working that you didn't even know existed!

Paleo favors shorter, more intense, strength-based workouts over lengthy cardio sessions. In fact, chronic cardio has been dubbed the exercise equivalent of whole grains! Too much cardio can be damaging to your entire system because it puts your body into a constant state of fight or flight. The results of such stress are an increase in cortisol levels and damage to your cells from inflammation and free radicals. In addition, to maintain such high levels of physical activity on a regular basis requires you to include an incredible amount of carbohydrates in your diet, and this causes damage to your body by messing with your insulin levels.

Paleo advocates that exercise should not feel like a cruel and inhumane form of torture where you feel constantly exhausted and sore, but rather it should be enjoyable and leave you feeling strong and energized. Rest and recovery is an important aspect of Paleo exercise. When it comes to exercise, more is not always better. Mainstream culture generally tends to equate more exercise with the ability to eat more. People are obsessed with losing weight and will employ whatever "tricks" they can to stave off the hunger that comes with calorie-restricted diets. How many times have you said, "Ooh I went for a run, so now I can eat that cake and it will cancel out?" I've lost count of how many times I have reasoned with myself in a similar fashion. Paleo fitness does not have weight loss as its primary goal—it's a fortunate consequence of following the right eating plan and becoming more active. Again, sustainability is key—getting stuck in a cycle of eating too much and then increasing the number of hours you spend at the gym is counterproductive, painful, and dangerous, because you are on the fast track to burn out and collapse. Your body needs days of rest for your muscles to recover. Now this doesn't mean vegging on the couch all day. Paleo fitness, just like the diet, requires a long-term commitment to caring for your body all the time. On rest days, it requires slow movement instead of intense strenuous exercise. So instead of lifting weights, go for a walk, stand up at work and do some stretches instead of sitting slumped over your desk all day—things like this that make movement a part of your routine constitute a rest day—it does not mean becoming a couch potato (or couch sweet potato if you want to be Paleo technical!). Focus on consistent physical activity to keep your muscles and body working optimally and always remember to work with your body, not against it!

Just as Paleo food can be tweaked and adapted to suit your own set of personal circumstances, so Paleo exercise is flexible as long as you operate within these broad guidelines. You need to find a program that works for you and fits in with the demands of your lifestyle, and that might require a little experimentation at first until you find something that's a good fit with your abilities and goals. Exercise should enhance your life, not dominate it!

At the end of the day, Paleo exercise should complement the diet and shouldn't require fancy equipment or a huge time commitment. Simple things you can incorporate into your daily life like walking instead of driving, taking the stairs instead of the elevator, and carrying your shopping bags to the car instead of pushing them in the cart will go a long way to kick-starting your Paleo exercise regime. Taking the dog for a walk on the weekends, going for a hike in the rough terrain of nature, or going for a short jog while your kids ride their bikes next to you are other good options. If you feel more comfortable with a more structured exercise program, there are many internet sites that post daily Paleo-friendly workouts that you can download and do in the comfort of your own home.

Embarking on an exercise program while on the Paleo diet requires you to ensure that you are eating sustainably. Don't skip meals in the hopes that it will help you to lose weight faster—that is not the goal of Paleo exercise. Always listen to what your body tells you it needs, and provide it in Paleo-friendly forms. Make sure you stay well-hydrated by drinking plenty of water, and try to include some starchy vegetables in your meals to power your workouts. I have included some delicious smoothie recipes in this book to replenish and revitalize your body after a workout—they are tried and tested and truly work wonders. So get active and wake up those muscles. Once you start, the rush is totally addictive, and, trust me, you will need some kind of exercise regime in place to work off all the yummy Paleo desserts!

STRESS

The sad and unfortunate reality is that we live in very stressful times. Our lives are fast-paced, and the result of that is that our stress levels have skyrocketed in recent years. How many times have you heard yourself utter the phrase, "if only I had a few more hours in the day?" If I had a dollar for every time I have said it, I would have been rich long ago!

Between the demands of work, family, and trying to hold onto a semblance of a social life, it's fair to assume that we do more in a day now than our forbearers probably did in a week! The result is nothing short of sheer exhaustion for many of us, and that equates to high levels of stress as we navigate through the sometimes insurmountable to-do list that just seems to get ever longer.

But what is stress, and exactly what does it do to our body? Stress is a disturbance of the body's state of homeostasis, or balance. It refers to any event where the demands made on an individual exceeds our adaptive resources—in other words, our ability to cope with said event. When we lose our ability to regulate ourselves to our inner or outer environment, we open ourselves up to disease. Stress harms the body in every imaginable way, and I could literally write an entire book on the harmful effects of stress, but for now I'm just going to summarize.

Basically, our adrenal glands secrete a hormone called cortisol that helps to regulate our response to stressors. Stressors can be obvious things like arguing with a spouse or friend, sitting in traffic, financial concerns, work concerns, your kids, impossible schedules, or any of the other challenges of modern life; or they can be not-so-obvious things like food intolerances, sickness, environmental toxins, gut problems, inflammation, and overtraining, which nevertheless still sound the alarm and cause the adrenals to pump out more cortisol. Symptoms of stress include but are not limited to mood swings, sleep disturbances, fatigue, headaches, depression, anxiety, sugar cravings, weight gain, irritability, decreased libido, dizziness, digestive complaints, weakened immunity, and therefore chronic sickness. Not a pretty picture I'm painting, is it?

Now, cortisol has a role to play in your normal day-to-day functioning. It should follow a certain pattern throughout the day, being high in the morning (to help you with that get-up-and-go feeling you need to start your day) and gradually decreasing through to the evening (so you are tired at bedtime and can sleep). Chronic and prolonged stress disrupts this natural rhythm of cortisol production in the body because every time you feel stressed, those adrenals pump out more cortisol to help you cope. The upheaval of the cortisol rhythm is what wreaks havoc in your body. Not only are your cortisol levels higher than normal, but they also tend to spike in the evening when they should be at their lowest, which affects our sleep, and I think we can all agree that lack of sleep is the slowest form of torture—EVER!

While the physical effects of stress are awful, the psychological impact of constantly feeling stretched too thin can simultaneously wreak havoc with your mental health. Negativity is like a festering sore, and before you know it, you will be spiraling down into the depths of depression and despair.

Do you remember what Paleo means? It means making a long-term commitment to your overall health and well-being. Since stress is something that can upset your state of balance and throw you off kilter, thereby affecting not only your short-term health, but leaving a lasting stamp on your long-term health, part of Paleo means making a commitment to manage your stress levels. You can eat like a perfect Paleoite and exercise regularly, but if you don't take care to manage your stress effectively, you are still going to be at risk for developing those nasty lifestyle diseases I keep telling you about—autoimmune issues, heart disease, diabetes, and hypothyroidism have all been linked to high levels of stress.

What I find quite amazing is that we will all make the effort to change what we eat or take pills to try to make ourselves feel better but seem to shy away from mitigating the harmful effects of stress. Stress is a modern reality, and that is a fact that we cannot get away from. We can play the ostrich and stick our heads in the sand, but it's not going to magically disappear because it is a pervasive modern problem, and I predict as we, the human race, continue to develop and progress, it is only going to get worse. I cannot stress enough how vital it is to get a proper stress management program into place as soon as possible.

Why are people so seemingly reluctant to get this aspect of modern life under control? Well it's quite simple really—it touches a nerve. We are so conditioned to be busy and productive that taking "me time" every day seems indulgent and unnecessary and (gasp) makes us appear lazy to our peers. It's about the person we want to put forward in the world. Under it all, people really do care what others think of them, and at the end of the day, it's far easier to make dietary changes than to change behavior. I also think that many people actually don't want to acknowledge the real feelings that are signaled by stress—feeling defeated and overwhelmed. Nobody wants to be the person who isn't coping when all your friends and family are multi-tasking machines capable of excellent time management and do it all with perfect make-up and a pair of six-inch heels to boot. I get it—stress management is difficult because it asks a lot of us and many of us actually don't have any more to give. We are all so entwined in the modern rat race that we actually don't know what to do with the thought of disengaging from it for a while and just slowing down and taking a step back. It's a constant GO GO GO lifestyle with no reprieve. The world we live in no longer values the self, and stress management asks us to prioritize exactly that. It's our modern existential crisis!

I have laid it all down on the line for you in this book, giving you the no-holds-barred truth throughout, and guys, I've got to lay down a little tough love here: If you are not going to engage in some stress management on a regular basis in whatever form best works for you, you are going to sabotage all the wonderful effort you are making with diet and exercise! And that's the truth of it. Managing

your stress is a crucial component to longevity and vital to achieving optimal health—it has become a modern necessity in the primal blueprint.

So because I care about your stress levels, here is a list of some effective stress-busting strategies to help you get those cortisol levels down and your stress under control. While it is virtually impossible to escape stress altogether, you can take steps to reduce the stress you are exposed to, and there are things you can do to try to limit the damage of the stress you do experience.

So let's look at the first kind—how do we go about avoiding unnecessary stress?

1. Avoid people who stress you out. You know who I mean—those drama queens who are simply just draining to be around. If you cannot avoid them altogether, limit the time you spend with them.
2. Know your own limits. You know what you can handle and what you realistically have time for, so don't take on new projects that are going to stretch you to the breaking point. There is a wonderful word in the English language—NO—learn it and use it!

3. Limit your exposure to the news. Let's face it, sometimes the news is just plain depressing. Other times, it is stressful. Constantly seeing stories about crime in your area is stressful and adds to your already burgeoning load. I'm *not* saying be uninformed, just limit your exposure to these kinds of stressors. Choose what you want to be exposed to; you don't have to know about everything that is happening in the world every day.

4. Pick your arguments—you don't have to fight every fight, and you don't always have to win or have the last say. Especially don't get sucked into fights on social media! They serve absolutely no purpose, and getting into a war of words with the increasing number of keyboard warriors out there does nothing to lower your levels of stress, because I can promise you nothing you might say is going to do anything to change the way they think or behave. Scroll past! Do not engage!

5. Escape the shackles of your to-do list. It does not all have to get done in one day. Prioritize. Spend some time considering exactly what needs to get done that day, and push the rest to the bottom of the list or simply scratch them off altogether—I mean really, does it matter if your shoe cupboard is color coordinated??

Now what about the kinds of stress we cannot avoid? Maybe you are going through a divorce or you have a high-stress job or you are nursing an ill parent or child. These kinds of situations are unavoidable in life and undoubtedly very stressful, so we need to learn how to limit the damage to our body.

1. **Change your perspective.** Stress oftentimes is a result of the meaning we assign to events in our lives; for example, being stuck in traffic every day on the way home from work can be a disaster that sends you into a spin and makes your already bad mood reach epic proportions, or you can think about it as a chance to reflect on your day. If you have kids in the car, it can be a wonderful opportunity to spend some quality time with them without any distraction. Your view of a situation can determine the stress factor. Think before you stress!

2. **Say goodbye to perfectionism.** Yes, all you type A's out there, I'm talking to you! Simply doing your best is good enough.

3. **Accept the things you cannot change.** Easier said than done, I know, but stressing about something you can do nothing about serves no purpose. Stop wishing your life were different—it does nothing but waste time and breed contempt for what you do have. Celebrate your blessings because, if you really think about it, you have many. Let go of what you cannot control. Being grateful for what you have can completely change your perspective in life and relieve a mountain of stress.

4. **Learn some deep-breathing techniques.** It has been shown to lower blood pressure quickly and helps to teach the body to handle stress better. Use this when you feel overwhelmed or anxious, and you will feel better.

5. **Talk.** Talking about your stressful situation with a close friend can help because it will likely give you a new perspective. Make sure you pick someone calm who will be receptive and practical. Simply getting your woes off your chest can do wonders for your stress levels. A good support system of friends and family is crucial to limiting the effects of stress.

6. **Become a time-management guru.** Poor time management leads to stress and feelings of being overwhelmed. When you are not on top of things, it is difficult to stay relaxed. Plan your day carefully with realistic expectations of your time. Remember—tomorrow is another day.

7. **Find your bliss.** It is essential to make time for some fun in your life. Whatever that may be, find something that you love to do, and do it with gusto. Here are some good ideas for fun and relaxation that are super stress busters:

- Take a yoga class
- Take a walk on the beach
- Lose yourself in a movie
- Meditate
- Get a massage
- Take a long, relaxing bubble bath

- Read a good book
- Get outside into the fresh air
- Go swimming
- Cuddle your pet
- Dance
- Listen to music

Stress management is one of the most important things we can do to safeguard our health, yet it is usually the thing that falls to the bottom of the list in our busy lives. Yes, life is stressful but that doesn't mean you have to be stressed. Your health should be the thing of foremost importance in your life, so change what you can, and don't become emotionally invested in things you cannot control. Put yourself first by saying NO THANKS to stress!

EATING OUT AND SOCIALIZING

We all have days where the thought of standing in the kitchen preparing a meal at the end of a long day sounds about as appealing as sticking a fork in your eye. There are times when you just want to go out, be served a delicious meal, and not have to worry about washing up afterwards. But now you are Paleo, and you had to say goodbye to restaurant dining along with your old life of bread, pasta, and yogurt—right?

WRONG! You could not be more wrong.

Paleo is not meant to be a life sentence of misery and deprivation—within reason, you should be able to enjoy all the activities you did prior to adopting the Paleo lifestyle, and that also means eating out when you feel like it. You CAN become a fully-fledged social butterfly—Paleo style! That's right, you too can enjoy a satisfying social life without deviating from your commitment to good health. Honestly, there is nothing worse than being the gooseberry at social gatherings who simply sits there sipping on a water and never sampling any of the food or, worse yet, Harry Hermit who always says "No" when invited out. Well, the good news is you don't have to be either. You can still enjoy eating out without fear that you are doing your body untold harm. It's time to let your hair down and venture out of your own dining room for a meal to remember.

The trick is to make it work for you, and by becoming schooled in a little bit of Paleo Street savvy, you too can enjoy fine dining worry-free. There is no denying that eating out and socializing when you follow the Paleo way can be a challenge, but it is not impossible if you know how. With a little bit of effort and planning, you can join your friends and family for a meal outside of your own house (gasp!) and still keep yourself firmly on the Paleo track. So if you are chomping at the bit for a night out, here's what you need to know.

With the rise in food allergies, intolerances, and sensitivities lately, as well as all the fad diets currently sweeping the world that exclude food groups or emphasize certain combinations, the restaurant industry has taken a bit of a knock. The world is now full of "fussy eaters" who don't eat this or that and seem to want the impossible when dining out. Fortunately, this has worked well in Paleo's favor, as there are now a number of restaurants who offer allergy-free meals as menu staples. Still others have dairy- and gluten-free options, and others cater to a specific style of eating. If restaurants wish to keep their clientele happy, they have to roll with the times and cater for the full spectrum of palates. Many places offer things like lettuce wraps or bun-less burgers next to their gluten and dairy counterparts. Certain restaurants offer an option where you can build your own meal, so you can ask for exactly what you want and request it to be prepared a certain way. So folks, consult your trusty oracle called Google and see if you can find a restaurant in your area that caters for allergies. There are also a number of organic restaurants that are springing up, and these would be good options for Paleo dining, too.

Social media is often also a wealth of information with many Facebook groups dedicated to rating restaurants and discussing the pros and cons of a place. Join one that services your area, enter in your question, and within minutes you will have people responding with personal experiences, both good and bad.

No establishment wants the bad press of someone having a reaction to their food, so generally most places are more than happy to accommodate special requests if you politely explain that you suffer from food allergies.

Once you have found a place you like, becoming a regular and building a relationship with the owners and staff is a sure-fire way to get the service you want (and giving good tips won't hurt either!). But however you choose to dine out (at one regular place or trying a variety of places), never be afraid to speak up—while nobody likes to be the wet blanket holding up the meal with a whole bunch of special requests, it is YOUR health at stake, and you have a right to ask for what you want and to know what you are putting in your body. When you are seated and handed menus, politely explain from the outset that you are dairy- and gluten-free, and ask if they can accommodate you. The chef might come and speak to you personally and prepare your meal for you exactly as you want it—bonus!

Probably the biggest issue when you eat out is that often you can't see all the food for yourself. Sauces, for example, are packed full of hidden ingredients. Soy sauce contains gluten, and tomato sauce is laden with sugar and preservatives. So unless you are sure that the people serving you and cooking your food are properly clued up on Paleo principles, it's a good idea to ask for the sauce on the side or simply omit it altogether. Curries and stews and that sort of fare can become problematic, too, as they are often thickened with wheat-based thickening agents. Sometimes omelets and scrambled eggs are made with milk, and things like burgers and crab/fish cakes can be full of bread crumbs. Now you are probably thinking, "Well that rules out much of the menu. What's left after you have eliminated all of that? I certainly didn't come out to order a grilled chicken breast and steamed broccoli!"

One of the easiest options, especially if you are on friendly terms with the restaurant staff, is to carry your own Paleo-friendly condiments with you. Coconut aminos are a great substitute for soy sauce, and you can make your own Paleo tomato sauce, BBQ sauce, chutney, and so forth. Then you can order your meat and add whatever takes your fancy that night. Understandably, not many people are comfortable doing this, and if you have to whip up a batch of BBQ sauce for your steak before you head out, it kind of defeats the purpose.

But don't despair, if that option is not for you, there are a number of "safe" alternatives that you can order without drawing unnecessary attention to yourself. Steaks, roasts, and meats are all okay to order. Simply pair them with extra veggies and/or salad and hold the starch (unless they have a sweet potato option). Seafood is always a good choice paired with crisp salad. Thai-style curries with a coconut milk base will be naturally Paleo-friendly. Stir-fries are also always a good bet, just hold the rice or noodles. With all these options, a simple request to cook your food in olive oil rather than vegetable oil will not be unreasonable. Sticking to ordering two or three side dishes instead of one main is also a good option, as the ingredients are usually straightforward. It's also nice to have a little taste of everything instead of choosing one meal only—YUM! One of my favorite meals to eat in a restaurant is salad. I can never quite get mine quite as delicious or as filling as the ones you get in a restaurant. To make it a complete meal, add some chicken or beef strips and ask for a simple olive oil and balsamic dressing—it does not get more Paleo than that!

See, Paleo eating out is totally doable. If you have the will, you can always find a way!

EATING ON THE GO

In all fairness, if you gave people a choice about eating healthy, nutritious food or existing on fast food full of empty calories, I'd bet the vast majority would choose to be healthy (bar the occasional trip to Mickey D's). Nobody can live on processed food exclusively because even the most hardened junk-food addicts, if they're brutally honest, will admit that they don't feel good when they eat that way all the time. The unfortunate reality is that many of us are victims of lifestyle and eat poorly because it's just the times we live in.

There is no doubt about it, times have definitely changed. The human race is busier than ever before. Work takes a central position in people's lives because, if you want to get ahead, you have to be prepared to put in the hours often at the expense of almost everything else. Ambition and success are valued, and progress has become an almost fanatical obsession.

Time is one of the major reasons people have given me for why they are tucking into a processed fast-food burger for lunch instead of a healthy chicken salad. "I just don't have time to cook," they choke out between big bites of chemical-ridden meat and wheat-stuffed buns covered in cheese with preservative-laden sauce dripping down their chins—sounds yummy, right?

While I don't dispute that time has become a real contributing factor to our unhealthy lifestyles, it might surprise you to learn that eating on the go is actually not all that difficult. Now granted, I do have a bit of OCD when it comes to being organized, but really all it takes is a little planning, and you can also eat on the go in our fast-paced world and still adhere to the Paleo way.

Snacking is seriously the lethal injection of all eating plans, not just Paleo, so the trick is to ensure that you always have a healthy alternative at hand to counteract the munchies when they strike. The reason most other diets are doomed is that the calorie restriction eventually gets you, and there is only so long you can fight hunger before you snap and give in. The key to Paleo is to never let yourself get so hungry that you lose all sense of reason! Keeping your body fueled with the right things at regular intervals will guarantee success on this journey called Paleo.

The section before has given you a few practical solutions to ordering out if you are stuck in a pinch, but if you prefer to make your own food, here are a few tips to ensure you are never stuck in a stare-down with a vending machine while the angel and devil engage in mortal combat on your shoulder.

1. The freezer is your best friend—for real! There are so many things that can be made ahead and frozen—meatballs, hamburger patties, muffins, soups, and so forth—and then just pulled out the night before to defrost for lunch/snack. All you have to do is set aside one day every month to cook in bulk, and voila—food at your fingertips when you need it.

2. Always over-cater—my husband likes to tease me that instead of cooking for a family of four, I could easily feed a family double that size, and while at first it might seem wasteful, that couldn't be further from the truth, because we always have enough for a wholesome Paleo meal for lunch the following day. Killing two meals at once halves the time you have to spend in the kitchen.

3. Always fall back on good old faithful salads—if you have meat left over from dinner, even better. It takes no more than ten minutes to throw a salad together, and it is one of the best things you can eat.

4. Become a smoothie queen (or king)—toss a whole bunch of fruits into the blender with a handful of ice cubes and a splash of coconut/almond milk. Decant into a flask and off you go out the door—easy as pie!

So toss your excuses out the door because with a little forethought and preparation, eating on the go is something that will become second nature to you as you become more immersed in the Paleo way of life.

GETTING YOUR KIDS ON BOARD
(AND PERHAPS A WAYWARD SPOUSE)

Embarking on any major lifestyle change is no easy feat, and in this regard, the Paleo diet is no different. For someone who has been raised on grains and dairy, excluding these products from your diet is hard and takes extraordinary patience, strength, and willpower. Paleo moms and dads, it's all in your delivery—you can make Paleo sound wonderful, or you can make it sound dreadful. Kids (bless them) can be stubborn little devils when they set their minds to something, and the trick is to know yours well. Know what makes them tick and know their weaknesses, then plan a strategic assault on all that's bad for them, and let Paleo take over without them even realizing it. Yes, yes, I know this all sounds very sneaky and a touch deceitful, but really sometimes outsmarting your kids takes more planning and preparation than invading a small country!

If you have older kids, you can try the well-reasoned approach of calm explanation about the pros and cons of the Paleo diet and why it is the way forward, and you would be guaranteed a reasonable measure of success with some kids. Some, on the other hand, are likely to mobilize the forces and embark on a resistance movement that will have you wishing you had never heard of the Paleo diet. Bad habits are hard to break, and older kids might have a tough time because they have been eating a certain way all their lives and grown used to it (also, let's face it, many of the things that are bad for you are actually quite delicious, and trying to convince your tween that carrots are better for him than the chocolate-drenched donut in his hand is going to take CIA-type negotiation skills!). Younger kids can be a bit more tricky, and you are likely to be staring down the business end of a hissy fit at every meal if you try to change too much too quickly. Honestly, there is nothing worse than fighting your child at every meal time. It's frustrating, it's stressful, and nobody wants to do it three times a day! Obviously, first prize is to never get them started eating all the wrong stuff in the first place, but this is no small feat especially in today's world where junk food is very much a norm. So from a mom who has done it successfully, here are my tips to stay sane as you transition your kids (and perhaps a reluctant spouse) onto this eating plan.

First and foremost always remember—slow and steady does the trick. Turning into a crazed sergeant major who purges the house from all offending contraband and then scrutinizes everything that goes into your kids' mouths is not going to win you any parent-of-the-year. Remember you are on the right path now, so rather do it in a way where your new lifestyle is likely to be embraced and maintained than all at once where you are likely to find an extensive stash of taboo foods in the back of your kid's closet. Going "cold turkey" and bombarding your kids with a whole lot of changes at once is seldom met favorably with children. Rather, try changing a few small things at a time and making the transition over a longer period. When you use the cold-turkey approach, your body goes into shock and responds with cravings in force like never before. They are also far less likely to keep up with it if it seems like a huge sacrifice. The only thing a cold-turkey approach to non-Paleo foods is going to achieve is to make them deliciously forbidden and infinitely more appealing! Instead, make one change at a time, and let your family get used to it before making the next change. Yes, this will take longer, but by allowing their bodies time to adjust to the changes, you are safeguarding against a major food rebellion! In terms of how you go about instituting these changes and in what order is strictly a matter of personal preference. There is no right or wrong way to make this transition. Do it in a way you and your family are most comfortable with and at your own pace. If you take a bit longer than your friend, well so what? You have been consuming Paleo banned foods all your life; a few more weeks is not going to make that much of a difference. Going Paleo can be an incredibly fun adventure if you keep your wits about you and approach it in a sensible manner.

What I did—and it worked like a charm—was to make Paleo versions of all my kids' and hubby's favorite meals first before I even breathed the word Paleo within the four walls of my house. I did this randomly over a few weeks, making sure to ask them if they enjoyed the food (which they always did). I knew it was the right time to come clean when, one Sunday morning, my hubby asked me for those awesome new banana pancakes I had been making for breakfast. I whipped up a batch and sat them all down around the table and explained what I had done and that I wanted us all to become Paleo. I told them what I had researched and filled them in on all the benefits. My kids did look a little wide-eyed at the idea of no more candy, and junk food ever, but once I told them that we could make our own Paleo candy, they were happy to at least give it a try. Now, while that worked for me, you might prefer to have the talk first and then show them that you can make Paleo versions of almost anything—this is undoubtedly the best way to prove to them that Paleo does not mean giving up any of your favorite foods. For example, Paleo French fries made with sweet potatoes are a sure hit, make sandwiches with Paleo bread, or make Paleo choc chip cookies, waffles, and pancakes—all firm kiddie (and grown-up) favorites.

Whichever way around you choose to do it, an absolute necessity is to educate your family so they understand exactly why the foods they have been eating have been damaging their bodies. Knowing the important underlying health concerns and dangers helps you all to keep your iron resolve when faced with a table full of desserts or when at a friend's house for a party and all the delicious snacks are screaming "EAT ME!!!" The Paleo way of life is not a punishment or set of imposed restrictions that should make you resentful that you are missing out. It is the informed choice to give yourself and your family one of the greatest gifts—health.

Another way to go about making the switch is to Paleofy one food group or meal at a time. Start with swapping out cereals for eggs at breakfast, then when they are happy, move onto Paleo snacks and so on. Alternatively, you can start by cutting out sugar, then dairy, and then gluten. It doesn't really matter which way you choose—you need to do what works for your family and your own personal set of circumstances. Whatever option you choose, do your best, but also know that setbacks along the way are to be expected. Don't let one minor setback (or even a major one) undermine or undo all the positive steps you have put in place. Just take it in your stride, carry on, and don't give up.

Getting your kids involved is another good option. Let them help you plan meals, and, if they are able, let them help you prepare them. Even young children can be given tasks to do in the kitchen that are safe and age appropriate. Yes, this might initially mean a bit more work for you, but keep your eyes on the prize—creating happy, healthy Paleo kids! Research has shown that children are far more likely to try something new if they have been a part of making it. This is a perfect opportunity to create family time out of necessity in our busy, fast-paced lives. Make it a daily routine to cook dinner as a family, get the kids involved in preparing their school snacks and lunches, and most importantly make it fun—sing, dance, laugh—find out about your kids' day and what's going on in their lives. Invaluable quality time while still being productive? Now that's what I'm talking about!

And last but certainly not least—get CREATIVE in the kitchen—probably the best advice I can give you! If you just stick with meat and veg for your mains and fruit in between, you are going to get bored faster than you can say "Paleo!" Don't be afraid to experiment and try new food and flavor combos—the more imaginative, the better! I promise you, some of the weirdest combinations produce the most incredible taste sensations ever. I remember the first time I looked for a Paleo chocolate pudding recipe online and found one with avocado as an ingredient—I nearly died! I thought "how gross!" Then curiosity got the better of me and I tried it out. Hands down the best chocolate pudding I have ever eaten! Avocados have such a mild flavor that they simply absorb the flavors of whatever you add to them, and their smooth, creamy texture was just perfect for a chocolaty pudding.

When you adopt this diet, it is a good idea to throw out all your preconceived ideas and notions about food, along with your bread and pasta, and enter the Paleo lifestyle as a tabula rasa. This way you can be open to every new culinary experience offered to you. This book is an excellent starting point, and there is a wealth of literature on this subject online and hundreds of thousands of different recipes to try. Paleo is very forgiving. The recipes are by their very nature versatile, as they have mostly been adapted from classic recipes anyway. If you don't like something, leave it out or swap it for an ingredient you do like.

I'm not going to tell you lies or sugar-coat anything (of course I'm not, I'm Paleo!)—transitioning your family to this way of life is going to be challenging and you will have bad days, but once it's done, you will never look back. You will appreciate every tantrum, screaming match, and fight about food when you watch your children refuse non-Paleo food in favor of healthy options—not to mention that you will be so proud it will feel like your heart is going to burst right out of your chest. So take the bull by the horns and start today—you won't regret it!

SHOPPING FOR PALEO

Shopping as a new Paleoite can be a daunting prospect. Our body seems to be hard-wired to crave those things that we have told it that it may not have, and while you detox the bad stuff out of your body, seeing it sitting temptingly on the shelves of the grocery store can crumble the resolve of even the strongest willed people in seconds. In the early days, it is very easy to fall off the wagon, so you need to implement some new routines before attempting to go to the shops.

The number one golden rule of Paleo shopping is to NEVER go to the shops when you are hungry—EVER! The candy will call out to you—I promise! The best thing to do is to set it up as routine that shopping always happens after a filling, wholesome, and nutritious Paleo meal because I can assure you if you go there hungry, by the time you reach the checkout, you will be halfway through your second caramel candy bar! You will suffer from guilt-induced shame and hate yourself for days afterwards while enduring severe mental self-flagellation where you call yourself all manner of ugly names. It would be SO much easier if they just had Paleo-friendly stores, wouldn't it?

Don't be discouraged—it won't be that hard all the time. As you become a seasoned Paleoite and start to actually feel the difference in your body, the temptations will lessen, and shopping will no longer be fraught with cravings and nerves. It's only hard in the beginning as your body becomes accustomed to a new way of eating. Also, as you get more experienced with this diet, you will learn how to satisfy your cravings in Paleo-friendly ways.

Paleo can become an expensive endeavor if you don't shop smart. Because this diet relies chiefly on consuming fresh produce, you can run a real risk of food going off before you have a chance to cook it if you don't plan properly. But if you are clever, it needn't break the bank and require you to take out a second mortgage on your home! Personally, I find the best way to shop for Paleo is weekly. That way your ingredients are always fresh, and you have minimal wastage especially if you have planned your meals in advance and drawn up a shopping list and a budget. When you set off to the shops, leave your credit card at home and make sure you have only enough money to buy what you need—this keeps impulse spending on non-Paleo items in check.

Now while you can find most Paleo staples in your local supermarket or health shop, for me there is no better place to shop for Paleo than your local farmers' market. Most markets run weekly and stock the freshest of fresh organic produce. While it is not an absolute requirement that your food is only organic, it is recommended to buy organic and free-range as often as possible. The commercially grown produce and commercially farmed meats are packed full of chemicals and hormones, and if you can it is naturally a better option to avoid these. As an added bonus, generally the people who sell at these markets are health nuts just like you and me, so you are not likely to find much junk food there. Consequently you won't be faced with all the perilous temptations of the supermarket that can be the death knell of your Paleo efforts. The farmers' market ticks all the boxes—fresh, weekly, organic—what more can you ask for?

And if all else fails—take someone stronger and with more willpower with you to do the shopping. That way if you start to deviate from the list, he or she can drag you out of the shop caveman style!

HOW TO TELL IF A RECIPE IS PALEO-FRIENDLY

To tell if a recipe is Paleo-friendly, you need to make sure you are educated in Paleo principles and Paleo foods. Paleo is huge at the moment, and there is no shortage of food-list resources of what you can and can't consume. The food lists in this book give you an excellent starting point, as I have listed the major foods that you can safely consume and those that are taboo. If a recipe calls for an ingredient that you are not certain of, a quick Google search should clear up the matter. Remember though, *"if in doubt, leave it out!"* There are many recipes out there that are borderline, because not all people follow Paleo to the same degree. Some people are much more relaxed and will cook with things that are not strictly Paleo. Again, how strict you want to be is entirely a personal matter.

Generally though, it is accepted that a stricter stance is adopted in the presence of diseases and specific food sensitivities or allergies. For everyone else, it is not necessary to turn into a food Nazi who questions the origins of every morsel of food that crosses your lips. This will make you and everyone around you miserable! Just being well-versed in the major points of the Paleo diet is enough to get by, and the fine-tuning relating to the more obscure ingredients will come with time, practice, and experience.

For me, more important than whether a specific recipe is Paleo is the question of how to go about converting it into a Paleo-friendly version that doesn't compromise on taste. Well, if you have done your homework, Paleofying most recipes is a matter of simple substitutions. Many contraband foods like mayonnaise, Worcestershire sauce, and tomato sauce have Paleo versions that are easy enough to find online, make, and substitute in. Most Paleo recipes are very versatile and incredibly forgiving, and you can play around and experiment with them without fear of major culinary disasters. Taking more complicated regular recipes and converting them is another story, of course—I once found a pizza recipe with Paleo "cheese" that someone must have spent absolute ages perfecting, and let's be honest, most of us don't have the time or the inclination to undertake such humongous culinary feats. And you run the risk of some serious kitchen mishaps if you don't get the quantities and combinations exactly right. This is especially true with baking. Having said this, though, if you are craving a particular dish, just ask Google for the Paleo version of it, and you are guaranteed to get results.

The single most important tool in deciding if a recipe is Paleo-safe is knowledge. Become a sponge for all things Paleo. Learn what you can and can't eat and which substitutions can be safely made. Know that soy sauce contains gluten, so tamari sauce is a better option, but coconut aminos are even better. Learn the facts so that they become second nature to you. It seems overwhelming in the beginning, but it's actually pretty easy once you get the hang of it.

5
WORKING THE 14-DAY MEAL PLAN

I don't know about you guys, but there is nothing I hate more than being told what to eat and when! I am straight up a "choices girl," and that is probably one of the reasons I have never been very good at traditional diets. "Eat 200 grams of tomatoes at 9:13 a.m."—no thanks! The truth is, the body craves what it does when it does for a reason—it needs it, plain and simple. So why do we ignore what our bodies tell us? This is why traditional diets fail time and again. You are forcing your body to eat a specific way at certain times, and let's face it, even the most delicious of meals when you don't feel like it or aren't hungry can feel like you are chewing on cardboard.

This is one more Paleo pro—it's not about deprivation, it's not about counting calories, and it's not about going without. It's entirely the opposite—

it's about fueling your body with exactly what it needs when it needs it. It's about becoming so tuned in to your own body that you never have to feel that light-headed dizziness associated with calorie restriction and starvation ever again.

When you really get into Paleo, I can guarantee that if you eat sensible portions (and we all know what those are) on a regular basis, you won't feel hungry. You won't feel like racing down the checkout aisle scoffing candy bars as you go—it simply won't be something you even think about anymore. That's right, when you are giving your body good, wholesome, nutritious food that keeps your blood sugar levels balanced, you will no longer experience those awful cravings that can make even the sanest of us lose our minds.

With that in mind, I have devised a pretty ingenious menu plan that leaves food choices entirely up to you. In addition, I have used a wide selection of ingredients, so there is something for every palate. The recipes are versatile, so you can feel comfortable making simple substitutions to suit your personal preferences if so desired, AND there are enough recipes to have something new at every meal for two whole weeks—awesome right?

I have thirteen breakfast recipes to tantalize your taste buds and get your days off on the right foot—full of energy for the day. Some do take a little longer to prepare, so try to keep those for the lazy weekend days when you are not rushing like mad to get to work.

Lunches I have divided up into seven salad recipes and seven lunches. The salads are filling enough to be a meal and include all kinds of yummy combinations to delight your palate—who said greens have to be boring?

There are fourteen dinners as well as fourteen side dishes—have fun mixing and matching and trying out different flavor combos. Where something pairs really well with a particular main, I have made a note to make this as easy as possible for you.

I have included fourteen snack recipes, most of which make more than a single portion, and all store really well for a few days if you take care to ensure they are stored correctly in airtight containers, so you can make a batch of a recipe and be good to go for a few days. For your other snack, simply munch on a piece of fruit or a handful of nuts to tide you over to your next meal.

There are seven dessert recipes (probably more than there should be, but I just couldn't decide). Proceed here with caution as they are so deliciously scrumptious that you will find it hard not to make one every night. "Paleo desserts," while made with healthy ingredients, does not automatically mean they are good to eat all the time. The ones I have chosen are incredibly decadent, and if you are going to be indulging all the time, I suggest you go out now and invest in a new pair of running shoes!

As an added bonus for all you gym junkies out there, I have included three smoothie recipes that are fantastic to have as an after-gym body booster. They are packed full of all the right things to replenish and revitalize your body after a hard workout. They are all high in protein without a single scoop of whey protein powder in sight—all natural and totally yummy to boot!

So without further ado, it's time to whet your appetite as you page through some amazing Paleo recipes. I will be completely gobsmacked if you haven't beaten a hasty path to the kitchen before you are halfway through the book. If these recipes don't sell you on Paleo, then I'm afraid nothing ever will. In fact, I guarantee you will be wondering why you didn't convert to this lifestyle years ago!

6
RECIPES

BREAKFAST

SPINACH AND SHROOM SOUFFLÉ

Yields: 4 Servings

INGREDIENTS:

2 teaspoons olive oil

8 shiitake mushrooms, finely chopped

1 onion, finely chopped

2 garlic cloves, minced

8 ounces baby spinach leaves, finely chopped

8 eggs, beaten

½ cup almond milk

½ cup pecans, finely chopped

2 teaspoons coconut oil

DIRECTIONS:

1. Preheat your oven to 350° F.
2. Heat up the olive oil in a large skillet and sauté the mushrooms, onions, and garlic until they are soft.
3. Now place everything, except the coconut oil and pecans, into a large mixing bowl and stir it together until it is thoroughly combined.
4. Lightly grease 4 individual ramekins with a little olive oil (depending on the size of your ramekins, you might need more than 4).
5. Divide the mixture between the ramekins and fill them almost to the top.
6. In a clean skillet, melt the coconut oil and lightly toast the chopped pecans over a medium-high heat.
7. When done, sprinkle them on the top of the soufflés and pop them into the oven.
8. Bake at 350° F for about 40 minutes or until a toothpick inserted into the middle comes out clean.
9. Remove from the oven and devour!

VEGGIE MEDLEY OMELET

Yields: 2 Servings

INGREDIENTS:

1 cup mixed vegetables (asparagus, mushrooms, onion, and broccoli)

4 slices free-range and nitrate-free bacon (2 per omelet)

4 eggs (2 per omelet)

2 tablespoons coconut milk

2 tablespoons olive oil, plus extra for drizzling

Salt and pepper to taste

DIRECTIONS:

1. First, roast your veggies: Preheat the oven to 400° F. Chop the veggies into bite-sized portions. Drizzle them with a little olive oil and season with salt and pepper to taste. Roast for 10 minutes or until tender.
2. In a nonstick skillet, cook the slices of bacon until they are crispy. Remove them from the pan and allow to cool down. When they are cool enough to handle, crumble them up and set them aside.
3. By now the veggies should be done, so remove them from the oven and allow them to cool down slightly while you make the eggs. Be sure to leave the oven on.
4. Whisk 2 eggs together with 1 tablespoon of coconut milk and season with some salt and pepper.
5. Heat up 1 tablespoon of olive oil in a nonstick skillet and pour in the eggs. Swirl the pan around so that the eggs coat the bottom of the pan evenly.
6. When the eggs are just starting to set, spoon half the roasted veggies over one half of the egg and sprinkle half of the crumbled bacon on top. Fold the "empty" side of the egg over the top of the roasted veggies and bacon, then pop it into the oven for about 2 minutes or until the top is nicely golden brown.
7. Repeat with the remaining ingredients to make the second omelet.

MISH-MASH HASH

Yields: 4 Servings

| This is a great little side to have with any breakfast recipe! |

INGREDIENTS:

3 tablespoons olive oil

2 sweet potatoes, peeled and diced

1 teaspoon paprika

1 teaspoon cumin

1 onion, diced

1 cup mushrooms, diced

1 teaspoon garlic, minced

4 eggs

Salt and pepper to taste

DIRECTIONS:

1. Add 2 tablespoons of olive oil to a large skillet and heat it up over a medium-high heat.
2. Add the sweet potatoes and spices, cover, and cook for 5 minutes, stirring often so the potatoes don't stick.
3. Add the mushrooms, onion, and garlic, and cook covered for another 5 minutes, stirring occasionally.
4. The hash is done when the sweet potatoes are crispy and brown and the other veggies are soft.
5. In a clean pan, add the remaining tablespoon of olive oil and heat it up over a medium heat. Crack the 4 eggs into the pan and cook for about 5 minutes or to your preference.
6. Divide the hash between 4 plates and top each with a fried egg.
7. Dig in!

BREAKFAST QUICHE

Yields: 4 Servings

This recipe is perfect for a weekend brunch!

INGREDIENTS FOR THE CRUST:

2 cups almond flour

2 tablespoons olive oil

2 tablespoons raw honey

Pinch of salt

INGREDIENTS FOR THE FILLING:

1 cup asparagus, cut into 1-inch pieces

1 onion, cut into wedges

½ cup mushrooms, sliced

8 slices free-range and nitrate-free bacon

6 eggs

4 tablespoons almond milk

2 tablespoons olive oil

1 teaspoon dried parsley

Salt and pepper to taste

DIRECTIONS:

The Crust:

1. Combine all the ingredients in a bowl and mix well. The mixture will be quite crumbly, but it will set when it cooks. Press the crust down in an even layer in the bottom of a lightly greased 9-inch pie dish.

The Filling:

1. Preheat the oven to 400° F.

2. Toss the asparagus, onion, and mushrooms with the olive oil, parsley, salt, and pepper, and pop it onto a baking tray in a single layer. Bake at 400° F for about 10 minutes or until the veggies have softened and are browning.

3. While the veggies cook, fry the bacon until it is cooked but not crispy. Remove from the heat and chop into pieces.

4. Spread the roasted veggies out on top of the pie crust and top with the bacon pieces.
5. Whisk the eggs and almond milk together and season with some salt and pepper. Pour the eggs over the veggies to the top of the crust.
6. Reduce the oven heat to 375° F. Carefully transfer the quiche to the oven and bake for 30—40 minutes or until the eggs are set.
7. Remove from the oven and allow to cool for 10 minutes, then slice and serve.

BAKED AVOCADO WITH EGG STUFFING

Yields: 2—4 Servings

Complete power breakfast—enjoy!

INGREDIENTS:

2 ripe avocados, halved and pits removed

4 eggs

4 free-range and nitrate-free bacon slices, diced

1 tablespoon freshly chopped parsley

1 teaspoon paprika

Salt and black pepper to taste

DIRECTIONS:

1. Preheat the oven to 425° F.
2. Scoop out some of the avocado flesh (if necessary) to make enough space for a whole egg to fit in.
3. Place 4 ramekins onto a baking tray and place 1 avocado half into each ramekin. Season each with a little salt and pepper.
4. Very carefully crack the eggs into the pit holes of the avocados, taking care to ensure that the yolks stay whole. Alternatively, if you are unsure of your egg-cracking ability, crack them into a bowl first and then gently transfer them to the avocados.
5. Sprinkle the eggs with the paprika.
6. Finally, top each one with diced bacon.
7. Place the tray into the oven and bake for 20 minutes—cooking time might vary slightly depending on the size of your eggs and avocados, so keep an eye on them. They are done when the egg whites are properly set.
8. Remove from the oven, sprinkle with freshly chopped parsley, and serve immediately.

PROSCIUTTO, SPINACH, AND TOMATO BRUSCHETTA

Yields: 2—4 Servings

INGREDIENTS FOR THE PALEO BAGUETTE:

2 cups almond flour

¼ cup finely ground flax seeds

2 tablespoons organic, gluten-free baking powder

1 teaspoon salt

1 teaspoon thyme

1 teaspoon garlic powder

½–1 cup boiling water

3 eggs, beaten

3 tablespoons organic apple cider vinegar

2 tablespoons raw honey

Olive oil as needed

INGREDIENTS FOR THE TOPPING:

1½ cups baby spinach leaves

8 cherry tomatoes, sliced

8 slices free-range prosciutto

Olive oil for drizzling

Balsamic vinegar for drizzling

DIRECTIONS:

The Baguette:

1. Preheat the oven to 350° F and line a French bread pan with some parchment paper. Mix the dry ingredients together in a bowl. Mix the wet ingredients (not the boiling water) together in a separate bowl. Pour the wet bowl into the dry bowl and mix, then slowly add the boiling water. Add enough that the dough comes together but is not too sticky to work with.

2. Shape the dough into a baguette and place it into the pan. Pour a little olive oil onto your hands and smooth out the top of the dough. This also allows a delicious golden, crunchy crust to form when the bread bakes. Bake for 1 hour, then allow to cool on a rack.

To Assemble:

1. Slice the baguette into 8 roughly equal, thick slices. Place the slices of baguette onto a baking tray and pop them into the oven until they are golden brown. Turn them over and repeat. Remove from the oven and allow them to cool slightly.
2. Arrange the baguette slices on your serving plate. Top each with some spinach leaves, a sliced cherry tomato, and a slice of prosciutto.
3. Finish off with a drizzle of olive oil and a drizzle of balsamic.

HASH BROWNS AND BACON

Yields: 2 Servings

Seconds are a must with this one!

INGREDIENTS:

8 slices free-range and nitrate-free bacon

2 cups sweet potato, grated

Salt and pepper to taste

1 cup onion, grated

1 egg

1 teaspoon garlic powder

DIRECTIONS:

1. Fry the bacon in a skillet until crispy. Set aside, reserving the bacon drippings.
2. In a bowl, combine the remaining ingredients and mix together well.
3. Fry about 2 tablespoons at a time of the mixture in the bacon fat until golden brown on each side.
4. Serve alongside your cooked bacon.

BLUEBERRY PANCAKES

Yields: 2 Servings

> **Pancakes the whole family will love! Can you imagine any bad day that starts this way?**

INGREDIENTS FOR THE BLUEBERRY JAM:

1½ cups blueberries

¾ cup raw honey

2 tablespoons freshly squeezed orange juice

1 teaspoon grated orange zest

INGREDIENTS FOR THE PANCAKES:

2 ripe bananas

4 eggs, beaten

1 teaspoon vanilla extract

¼ teaspoon cinnamon

Maple syrup for drizzling

DIRECTIONS:

The Jam:

1. Crush the blueberries with a potato masher, and then put them into a saucepan with the rest of the ingredients.
2. Bring the mixture to a boil over a medium heat, making sure to stir frequently so it doesn't stick. Allow to boil, stirring, for 20 minutes until it has thickened.
3. Remove from the heat and allow to cool down, then spoon the mixture into a clean jar and chill it in the fridge while you make the pancakes.

The Pancakes:

1. Mash the bananas very well with a fork until all the lumps are gone, then stir in the eggs, vanilla, and cinnamon.
2. Heat up a nonstick skillet over a medium heat. Drop 2 drops of olive oil into the pan and swirl them around.
3. Drop spoonfuls of the mixture into the pan and allow to cook until they are golden brown on both sides.
4. Place the warm pancakes onto your plate, drizzle them with a little maple syrup, and top with blueberry jam.

FRUIT SALAD WITH CINNAMON PIZZA

Yields: 4 Servings

INGREDIENTS FOR THE CINNAMON PIZZA:

1 cup almond flour

¼ cup ground flax seeds

1 egg

3 tablespoons ghee

1 tablespoon cinnamon, plus extra for sprinkling

1 tablespoon coconut palm sugar, plus extra for sprinkling

INGREDIENTS FOR THE FRUIT SALAD:

2 cups strawberries, quartered

2 cups pineapple, chopped

2 cups kiwi, chopped

1 cup blueberries

INGREDIENTS FOR THE DRESSING:

Juice of 2 limes

¼ cup raw honey

2 tablespoons freshly chopped mint

DIRECTIONS:

The Cinnamon Pizza:

1. Preheat the oven to 300° F and line a baking tray with some parchment (you might need to use 2).
2. Mix all the ingredients together in a bowl until it forms a ball. Place the ball between two pieces of parchment and roll it out into a circle shape about ⅛-inch thick.
3. Peel back the top layer of parchment and use a pizza cutter to cut slice shapes out of the dough. Place them onto the prepared baking tray, and sprinkle them with extra cinnamon and sugar.
4. Bake for 20 minutes until crispy.

The Fruit Salad:

1. Place all the fruit into a bowl and mix.

The Dressing:

1. Whisk the raw honey and lime juice together, then stir in the mint.

To Serve:

1. Pour the dressing over the salad and toss well. Serve with cinnamon pizza slices on the side.

CHORIZO AND BACON BREAKFAST PIZZA PIE

Yields: 2 Servings

You won't be able to help yourself!

INGREDIENTS FOR THE BASE:

1 cup tapioca flour

⅓ cup warm water

⅓ cup plus 2 tablespoons palm
shortening

1 egg

3 tablespoons ground flax seeds

3 tablespoons coconut flour

1 teaspoon baking powder

½ teaspoon salt

INGREDIENTS FOR THE TOPPING:

Paleo tomato sauce, as needed

½ an onion, thinly sliced

½ cup sliced mushrooms

1 chorizo sausage, partially cooked and
sliced

4 slices free-range and nitrate-free
bacon, lightly cooked and diced

2 eggs

DIRECTIONS:

The Base:

1. Preheat the oven to 350° F.
2. Place all the dry ingredients into a bowl, then pour in the warm water and mix well. Add the palm shortening and egg, and mix again.
3. Roll the dough into a ball—it will be a little sticky. Now halve the ball and place each smaller ball between 2 pieces of parchment and roll them out to ⅓-inch thickness. Line a baking tray with parchment paper and sprinkle it with some tapioca flour.
4. Place the 2 pizza bases onto the prepared tray and bake them for 10 minutes.

To Assemble:

1. Remove the bases from the oven. Spread a layer of tomato sauce on top of the base, and then arrange the onion slices in a single layer on top.

2. Build your pizza now from the outside in so that your egg has a space to sit in. Mix the mushroom, chorizo, and bacon into a bowl. Divide it in half and place the mixture in a circle around the outer two thirds of the base.

3. Crack the egg into the center of each pizza and pop it back into the oven for about 20 minutes until the eggs are set.

BREAKFAST BURGERS

Yields: 2 Servings

A new and delicious way to enjoy breakfast!

INGREDIENTS:

½ pound pork sausage meat

¼ pound free-range and nitrate-free bacon, chopped

4 tablespoons ghee

4 large eggs

Salt and pepper to taste

Olive oil for greasing

½ cup water

1 handful of baby spinach leaves

2 slices onion

2 slices tomato

DIRECTIONS:

1. Mix the sausage meat with the bacon.
2. Grease the inside of a 3½-inch cookie cutter with some olive oil. Place it on a plate and fill it with half the meat mixture. Press the meat down to form an even layer inside the cutter. This is going to be your burger patty.
3. Heat up 1 tablespoon of ghee in a skillet and add the patty (with the cutter on) to the pan. Allow it to cook over a medium heat until the patty starts to shrink away from the sides, then remove the cutter and turn the patty over. Cook until both sides are golden brown and the meat is done through the center. Repeat with the other half of the mixture.
4. Now grease two 3½-inch cookie cutters with olive oil. Crack 2 eggs into 2 small bowls and pierce the yolks with a fork.
5. Heat a clean nonstick skillet over medium and add a tablespoon of ghee. Place the 2 cookie cutters into the pan and gently pour an egg into each cutter. Add half the water to the pan outside the cutters, cover, and allow to cook until the eggs are cooked through.

6. Remove the pan from the heat and slide a spatula underneath each cutter to remove them safely from the pan. Place them on a plate, and then remove the cutter from around the egg. Repeat with the other 2 eggs—these will be the "buns."

To Assemble:

1. Place one eggy bun on a plate. Top it with some spinach leaves, then add the patty. Place one slice of onion and tomato on top of the patty and season with some salt and pepper before adding the other eggy bun on top. Assemble the second one the same. You can add any sauces or burger filling you like to these—they are totally customizable!

TROPICAL FRUIT CEREAL

Yields: 6 Servings

INGREDIENTS:

1½ cups pineapple, cubed

8 dates, pitted and chopped

¼ cup raw honey

¼ cup orange juice, freshly squeezed

2 tablespoons lime juice, freshly squeezed

1 tablespoon vanilla extract

1 tablespoon cinnamon

½ cup coconut oil, melted

2 cups coconut flakes

1 ½ cups slivered or chopped almonds

1 cup macadamia nuts, roughly chopped

1 cup cashew nuts, roughly chopped

½ cup sunflower seeds

½ cup pumpkin seeds

1 tablespoon orange zest

1 tablespoon lime zest

½ teaspoon salt

1 cup raisins

DIRECTIONS:

1. Add the following to your blender and process to a liquid: pineapple, dates, raw honey, orange juice, lime juice, vanilla extract, and cinnamon. Now pour in the melted coconut oil and blend until smooth.
2. Line 2 baking trays with parchment paper and preheat the oven to 250° F.
3. In a large bowl mix together the following: coconut flakes, almonds, macadamia nuts, cashews, sunflower seeds, pumpkin seeds, raisins, orange zest, lime zest, and salt.
4. Spoon the wet mixture from the blender into the bowl and mix well. Spread half the mixture out in a single layer on each tray and place them into the oven to bake for 2 hours. Stir the cereal every 20 minutes or so to ensure it cooks evenly and doesn't burn.
5. When the cereal is golden brown, remove the trays from the oven and allow them to cool down completely.
6. Mix in the raisins and store in an airtight container until needed.
7. Serve in a bowl with some almond milk for a quick breakfast!

FRENCH TOAST PALEO STYLE

Yields: 2 Servings

INGREDIENTS:

1 large eggplant

1 teaspoon salt

3 eggs

½ teaspoon vanilla extract

½ teaspoon cinnamon

Ghee to fry

Maple syrup to serve

DIRECTIONS:

1. Peel the eggplant and cut it into slices. Place the slices in a colander in the sink and sprinkle with salt. Leave to drain for 10 minutes. Pat the eggplant slices dry with a kitchen towel and set aside on a plate. Use a fork to poke a few holes into the slices so the egg mixture can get inside.
2. Whisk the eggs, vanilla, and cinnamon together in a bowl.
3. Place the eggplant slices into the bowl of egg and make sure they are evenly covered. Leave for 5 minutes.
4. Heat up a little ghee in a skillet and gently fry the eggplant slices over a medium heat until they are golden brown on each side.
5. Serve drizzled with maple syrup and your favorite French toast side (bacon, fruit, or BOTH!).

SNACKS

PEACH AND CITRUS MUFFINS

Yields: 1 dozen

Perfect for a mid-morning snack!

INGREDIENTS:

4 cups almond flour

1 teaspoon baking soda

¼ teaspoon salt

2 cups peaches, peeled and chopped

¼ cup raw honey

¼ cup ghee, melted

6 eggs

4 tablespoons orange juice

1 tablespoon orange zest

DIRECTIONS:

1. Preheat the oven to 325° F and grease a muffin tray well or line it with paper liners.
2. Mix all the dry ingredients together in a bowl.
3. Mix all the wet ingredients in another bowl.
4. Pour the wet ingredients into the dry bowl and stir well, then gently stir through the chopped peaches.
5. Fill each muffin cup almost to the top.
6. Bake in the oven for 30 minutes or until a toothpick inserted in the middle comes out clean.
7. Allow to cool in the pan for 10 minutes, and then transfer to a wire rack to cool completely.
8. Store in an airtight container and eat as desired.

COCONUT CRAB CAKES

Yields: 12 Cakes

INGREDIENTS:

1 cup almond flour

2 cups shredded coconut

1 pound crab meat

¼ cup spring onions, sliced thinly

¼ cup red pepper, diced finely

1 egg

4 tablespoons Paleo mayonnaise

1 teaspoon freshly grated ginger

1 teaspoon finely grated lime zest

Salt and pepper to taste

Olive oil for frying

DIRECTIONS:

1. Mix ½ cup almond flour and ½ cup shredded coconut with the rest of the ingredients. Mix gently so as not to break up the crab meat too much.
2. Divide the mixture into 12 patties, place them on a plate, cover and refrigerate for 45 minutes.
3. Mix the remaining coconut and almond flour together and place the mixture in a shallow dish. Coat the crab cakes in the "crumbs" and set aside.
4. Heat up some olive oil in a large skillet over a medium heat and fry the crab cakes in batches until they are golden brown and cooked through.
5. Remove from the oil and set on some kitchen towels to drain and cool.
6. Once cool, refrigerate until needed. They will hold in an airtight container in the fridge for 3 days.
7. Eat as desired!

FRUIT ROLLS

Yields: 10 Servings

This snack is great for adding to children's lunch boxes!

INGREDIENTS:

1 cup apples, peeled, cored, and roughly chopped

1 cup peaches, peeled, pitted, and roughly chopped

1 cup raspberries, roughly chopped

1 cup pears, peeled, pitted, and roughly chopped

2 cups water

2 teaspoons lemon juice

1 tablespoon raw honey

1 teaspoon cinnamon

DIRECTIONS:

1. Preheat the oven to 140° F and line a baking tray with parchment paper.
2. Place the fruit and water into a pot and bring to a simmer over a medium heat. Cover the pot and leave for 10 minutes. Remove the lid and stir the fruit, then mash it to a pulp with a potato masher.
3. Add the lemon juice, raw honey, and cinnamon, and mix well to combine. Simmer uncovered for another 10 minutes or until the mixture starts to thicken.
4. Transfer the mixture to the blender and pulse until smooth. Taste and adjust the lemon juice, cinnamon, or raw honey quantities if desired.
5. Spread the mixture in an even layer onto the baking tray. It should be about ¼-inch thick. Place in the oven overnight to dry out. The fruit rolls are ready when they are no longer sticky.
6. Remove from the oven and cut into even-sized portions. Now roll each portion up in some parchment paper and store in the fridge in an airtight container until needed.

APPLE AND BLUEBERRY NACHOS

Yields: 4 Servings

INGREDIENTS FOR THE TOFFEE CARAMEL:

1 cup coconut milk

½ cup coconut palm sugar

2 tablespoons water

1 tablespoon lemon juice

1 teaspoon vanilla extract

⅛ teaspoon salt

INGREDIENTS FOR THE NACHOS:

¼ cup almond butter

2 tablespoons raw honey

1 tablespoon almond milk (or more)

4–6 apples, cored and sliced into wedges

½ cup blueberries

¼ cup shredded coconut

¼ cup dark chocolate (70–90% cocoa), grated

DIRECTIONS:

The Toffee Caramel:

1. Place all the ingredients into a saucepan, whisk them together well, and heat them gently over a medium heat until boiling. Make sure to stir frequently to avoid burning. Continue to bubble gently until the liquid is dark and has thickened, then remove from the heat and allow to cool down to room temperature. Store in an airtight container and refrigerate overnight.

The Nachos:

1. Whisk the almond butter with the raw honey, and add the almond milk to thin it out a little.

2. Arrange the apple slices on your serving plate, scatter the blueberries over the top, and sprinkle with the shredded coconut and grated chocolate.

3. Drizzle with the almond butter mixture and finally top with lashings of scrumptious toffee caramel.

SUPER EASY SOUP SNACK

Yields: 2 Servings

> **Comfort food for when you need a pick-me-up!**

INGREDIENTS:

1 tablespoon olive oil

1 onion, chopped

1 garlic clove, mashed

¼ teaspoon grated ginger

2 sweet potatoes, peeled and chopped

4 carrots, peeled and chopped

4 cups organic chicken stock
   (more if you prefer a thinner soup)

Salt and black pepper to taste

DIRECTIONS:

1. Heat up the olive oil in a soup pot over a medium heat. Add the onions, garlic, and ginger and sauté until the onions are nicely browned.

2. Add the sweet potatoes and carrots, and cook for a further 5 minutes, then pour in the chicken stock, cover, and cook on low for 2 hours or until the vegetables are soft.

3. Using an immersion blender, blitz the soup until smooth, adding more water or stock until you achieve your desired consistency.

4. Season with salt and black pepper to taste.

5. Serve piping hot, sip, and relax.

SNACK BARS

Yields: 1 Dozen

INGREDIENTS:

3 ripe bananas

1½ cups almond flour

¼ cup arrowroot powder

¼ cup walnuts, chopped

¼ cup almonds, chopped

¼ cup cashews, chopped

¼ cup dried cranberries

¼ cup raisins

¼ cup sunflower seeds

¼ cup toasted pumpkin seeds

1 tablespoon vanilla essence

DIRECTIONS:

1. Mash up the bananas well with a fork (it is okay if there are lumps).
2. Add the flour and arrowroot powder and stir well, then stir in the rest of your ingredients and mix until well blended.
3. Grease a baking tray with a little olive oil and spread the mixture out into an even layer, pressing it down with a spatula.
4. Bake in a 275° F oven for about 40 minutes or until the edges are turning golden.
5. Remove from the oven and allow to cool slightly, then slice into bars.
6. Store in an airtight container in the fridge and eat as necessary.

SPICY SEEDS

Yields: About 2 cups

Be warned—super addictive!

INGREDIENTS:

2 cups pumpkin seeds, cleaned and dried

¼ cup olive oil

4 jalapeño peppers, chopped

½ tablespoon paprika

½ tablespoon garlic powder

1 teaspoon sea salt

DIRECTIONS:

1. Preheat the oven to 350° F and line a baking tray with some parchment.
2. Toss all the ingredients into a bowl and mix together well with your hands, ensuring the spices are evenly distributed.
3. Lay the seeds out in a single layer on the baking tray and pop it into the oven for 20 minutes, stirring every 5 minutes.
4. Keep an eye on the oven, as these can burn very quickly.
5. Once the seeds are cooked, remove the tray from the oven and allow them to come to room temperature.
6. Place into an airtight container and grab a handful whenever a snack attack strikes.

PRIMAL TRAIL MIX

Yields: 10 Servings

Great to take on a hike, or keep a stash in your bag!

INGREDIENTS:

1 cup almonds

½ cup cashews

½ cup toasted coconut flakes

½ cup pumpkin seeds

½ cup sunflower seeds

½ cup golden raisins

½ cup dried pineapple

½ cup dried apricots, chopped

½ cup dried cranberries

DIRECTIONS:

1. Mix the ingredients in a bowl and store in an airtight container.
2. Help yourself when the hunger strikes.

CAULIFLOWER STICKS

Yields: 2 Servings

INGREDIENTS:

1 cauliflower, stem removed and
   cut into florets

1 tablespoon oregano

½ tablespoon basil

1 tablespoon onion powder

1 teaspoon garlic powder

½ teaspoon cumin

½ teaspoon red pepper flakes

2 eggs

DIRECTIONS:

1. Preheat the oven to 425° F and lightly grease a baking tray with a little olive oil.

2. Place the cauliflower florets in a microwaveable dish and microwave for 10 minutes.

3. Place the cauliflower into the blender and pulse until smooth. Put into the fridge to cool down completely.

4. Now stir in the rest of the ingredients until thoroughly mixed.

5. Spread the mixture out on the baking tray until it is in an even layer about ½-inch thick.

6. Place in the oven for 25 minutes or until it starts to brown.

7. Remove from the oven, cut into sticks, and turn the sticks over.

8. Turn the oven up to 500° F and return the sticks to the oven to brown and get crispy.

TERIYAKI BEEF JERKY

Yields: 6 Servings

INGREDIENTS:

3 pounds beef flank steak

¼ cup coconut aminos

3 garlic cloves, minced

1 tablespoon salt

2 teaspoons cumin

1 teaspoon cinnamon

½ teaspoon white pepper

DIRECTIONS:

1. Using a sharp knife, slice the beef into ¼-inch strips.
2. Place the rest of the ingredients in a microwave-safe dish and microwave for 30 seconds on high to activate the spices.
3. Place beef into the marinade and refrigerate overnight to infuse the meat with the flavors.
4. The next day, preheat the oven to 170° F and lay the beef strips on a baking tray.
5. Bake for 12 hours until the meat has dried out.
6. Remove from the oven and allow to cool uncovered before storing in an airtight container in the fridge.

PALEO PROTEIN BALLS

Yields: 12 Servings

> ## The perfect little post-workout snack!

INGREDIENTS:

4 prunes, pitted

1 cup almonds

½ cup roasted, unsalted macadamia
    nuts

2 tablespoons raw honey

2 tablespoons coconut oil, melted

¼ cup strawberries, diced

¼ cup raspberries, diced

½ cup shredded coconut

DIRECTIONS:

1. Place the prunes into the blender and pulse until it forms a paste.
2. Add the nuts and pulse until they are finely chopped.
3. Now add the raw honey and coconut oil, but stop the blender as soon as it is incorporated.
4. Transfer the mixture to a bowl and stir in the strawberries and raspberries.
5. The mixture is quite sticky, so you have to work carefully when forming the balls. It is helpful to use an ice-cream scoop so the balls are a uniform size and then gently roll the mixture between your palms.
6. Once the balls are formed, roll them in the shredded coconut and place them on a parchment-lined baking tray in the fridge to set.

SALTED ROSEMARY CRACKERS

Yields: 2—4 Servings

INGREDIENTS:

2½ cups almond flour

2 eggs

3 tablespoons ghee, chopped

2 tablespoons dried rosemary (or to taste)

Sea salt to taste

DIRECTIONS:

1. Place the almond flour and eggs into your blender and process until combined, then add the ghee and process until just combined.
2. Remove from the blender and stir in the rosemary.
3. Form the mixture into a ball and roll it out between two sheets of parchment to your desired thickness.
4. Remove the top layer of parchment and place dough onto a baking tray parchment side down.
5. Sprinkle the top with some sea salt and bake in a 350°F oven until golden brown.
6. Remove from the oven and allow them to cool down before cutting them into squares.
7. Store in an airtight container.
8. Munch and enjoy on their own or with some guacamole!

BANANA CHIPS

Yields: 2 Servings

INGREDIENTS:

2 bananas

Juice of 1 lemon

2 teaspoons cinnamon

DIRECTIONS:

1. Preheat the oven to 200° F and line a baking tray with parchment paper.
2. Cut the bananas diagonally into thin slices.
3. Coat the slices in lemon juice and lay them onto the baking tray.
4. Sprinkle them as generously as you like with cinnamon and bake until they are crispy, turning them every 30 minutes.
5. When they are done, allow to cool and then store in an airtight container.

PALEO PORK RINDS

Yields: 2—4 Servings

INGREDIENTS:

¼ pound free-range pork skin

Salt to taste

Paprika to taste

Garlic powder to taste

DIRECTIONS:

1. Preheat the oven to 325° F and line a baking tray with some parchment.
2. Toss the pork skin with the spices, making sure the skin is well coated in flavoring.
3. Pop it in the oven for about 2 hours. Keep an eye on it, as you want it nice and crispy, but if you leave it too long it will become very hard.
4. Remove the tray from the oven.
5. Try to wait until they are cool before tucking in—pure torture!
6. There are various ways to treat the rinds, depending on the look you want. For uniformity, slice the raw rind into strips before cooking; if you'd prefer a more rustic look, break up the skin after it has been cooked and cooled.

LUNCH

SPINACH AND ZUCCHINI FRITTERS WITH AVOCADO SPREAD

Yields: 2—4 Servings

Simple to make and satisfying to eat!

INGREDIENTS FOR THE FRITTERS:

2 zucchini, washed, ends trimmed, and grated

½ cup baby spinach leaves, very finely chopped

¼ cup fresh basil, chopped

¼ cup almond flour

⅛ cup fresh oregano, chopped

2 eggs

1 tablespoon grated lemon zest

½ teaspoon crushed garlic

½ teaspoon onion powder

Salt and black pepper to taste

Olive oil for frying

INGREDIENTS FOR THE SPREAD:

1 ripe avocado

½ teaspoon onion powder

1 teaspoon lemon juice

¼ cup finely chopped dill

2 free-range and nitrate-free bacon slices—cooked crisply and crumbled

DIRECTIONS:

The Fritters

1. Place grated zucchini in a colander over the sink. Sprinkle with ½ teaspoon of salt and allow the liquid to drain out.

2. Move the zucchini into a kitchen towel and wring to remove any excess moisture. Place into a bowl with the remainder of the ingredients and mix well.

3. Heat up a little olive oil in a skillet over a medium heat and carefully drop about 2 tablespoons at a time of the mixture into the hot pan. Make sure to space your fritters a few inches apart so they don't stick as they

cook. Cook until both sides are golden brown. Continue to cook until all the zucchini mixture is used up, adding more oil as necessary.

The Spread

1. Mash the avocado well with a fork. Stir in the onion powder, lemon juice, and dill and mix well. Lastly, add the crumbled bacon and mix gently.

2. To eat: Spread some avocado mixture on top of a warm fritter—die and go to heaven!

ROASTED VEGETABLE "COUSCOUS" WITH FRUIT CHUTNEY

Yields: 2—4 Servings

INGREDIENTS FOR THE VEGETABLE "COUSCOUS":

2 cups butternut squash, peeled and cut into 1-inch cubes

1 red onion, cut into 1-inch cubes

2 zucchini, cut into 1-inch cubes

1 red pepper, cut into 1-inch cubes

1 yellow pepper, cut into 1-inch cubes

2 garlic cloves, minced

3 tablespoons olive oil

2 tablespoons toasted almonds, slivered

(garnish)

2 tablespoons freshly chopped cilantro

2 teaspoons cumin

1 cup organic vegetable stock

4 cups cauliflower "couscous"—pulse the cauliflower in the blender until it resembles couscous

Salt and pepper to taste

Juice of ½ a lemon

INGREDIENTS FOR THE FRUIT CHUTNEY:

1 cup dried apricots, soaked in water for an hour

¼ cup apple cider vinegar

½ cup dates

¼ cup water

2 tablespoons finely grated ginger

2 tablespoons raw honey

¼ teaspoon salt

DIRECTIONS:

The Vegetable Couscous

1. Preheat the oven to 400° F and place the cubed vegetables on a baking tray in a single layer. Drizzle with 2 tablespoons of olive oil and season with some salt and pepper.

2. Place in the oven for 20 minutes or until the vegetables are roasted but tender. Stir occasionally during the cooking time.

3. Heat up the remaining tablespoon of olive oil in a large skillet and add the garlic and cumin. Cook, stirring continuously, for 2 minutes or until fragrant, then pour in the vegetable stock and bring it to a boil.
4. Add the roasted vegetables to the skillet and then the cauliflower "couscous." Give it a good stir and then remove it from the heat. Cover the pot and allow it to stand for 5–10 minutes. The residual heat will cook the cauliflower until it is tender.
5. Remove the lid and stir through with a fork, then add the almonds and cilantro. Squeeze over the lemon juice and run the fork through gently to mix everything well.

The Chutney

1. Drain the apricots and place them into a saucepan with the apple cider vinegar, and bring it to a boil over a medium heat. Reduce the heat and allow it to simmer for 10 minutes or until all the vinegar has evaporated.
2. Stir in the remaining ingredients and allow to simmer until the chutney has thickened, stirring occasionally. Use the back of a wooden spoon to break up the apricots and dates until they are in chunky pieces (or to your desired consistency).
3. When the chutney is thickened, transfer it to a serving bowl and allow to cool down (you can speed this up by popping it in the fridge for 15 minutes).
4. Serve the vegetable couscous with a generous dollop of chutney on the side.

ORIENTAL STIR FRY

Yields: 4 Servings

INGREDIENTS:

1 teaspoon garlic, minced

1 teaspoon ginger, grated

1 red onion, sliced

1 pound beef, cut into strips

1 cup carrots, julienned

8 shiitake mushrooms, sliced

½ cup cashews, roughly chopped

½ cup red cabbage, shredded

1 cup bok choy cabbage, shredded

1 cup broccoli florets

1 red pepper, julienned

¼ cup vegetable broth

1 tablespoon raw honey

¼ cup coconut aminos

1 tablespoon water

1 tablespoon sesame seeds (garnish)

1 tablespoon sesame oil

DIRECTIONS:

1. Heat the oil up in a wok or a large skillet and add the garlic, onion, ginger, and beef. Sauté for 2 minutes on high, then add the carrots, mushrooms, cashews, cabbage, broccoli, and red pepper, and cook for a further 2 minutes.
2. Whisk the broth, raw honey, coconut aminos, and water, pour it over the veggies, and cook on high for another 2 minutes.
3. Remove from the heat, sprinkle with sesame seeds, and serve immediately.
4. This is a terrific stand-alone dish, but you can serve it over cauliflower rice or spaghetti squash if you like.

SIMPLE SHRIMP "TACOS" WITH AVOCADO AND GRILLED ONIONS

Yields: 4 Servings

Tacos with a twist!

INGREDIENTS FOR THE TACO SEASONING:

1 teaspoon paprika

1 tablespoon ground cumin

½ teaspoon dried oregano

1 tablespoon chili powder

¼ teaspoon garlic flakes

¼ teaspoon garlic powder

½ teaspoon onion powder

½ teaspoon crushed red pepper flakes

1 teaspoon black pepper

1 teaspoon salt

INGREDIENTS FOR THE TACOS:

2 tablespoons ghee

1 small onion, sliced

1 pound medium shrimp, peeled, deveined, and rinsed

2 tablespoons Taco Seasoning (Paleo-friendly)

1 head butter lettuce (or other leaf lettuce)

1 avocado, sliced

Handful of cilantro, chopped

Hot sauce, Paleo-approved (optional)

DIRECTIONS:

1. Melt 1 tablespoon of the ghee in a skillet over a medium-high heat.
2. Add the onions and sauté until they are just starting to brown. Remove from the heat and set aside for later.
3. Melt the remaining ghee in the same skillet.
4. Toss the shrimp with 2 tablespoons of the Taco Seasoning and cook the skillet for 1—2 minutes per side.
5. Assemble tacos by placing the shrimp in a piece of lettuce and top with some sautéed onion, an avocado slice, some hot sauce, and chopped cilantro.

TILAPIA WRAPS WITH FRUITY SALSA

Yields: 4 Servings

INGREDIENTS FOR THE TILAPIA:

2 tilapia fillets

Juice of 1 lemon

1 teaspoon ground cilantro

1 teaspoon dried basil

½ teaspoon garlic powder

Salt and pepper to taste

INGREDIENTS FOR THE WRAPS:

8 egg whites

½ cup almond flour

¼ cup water (add a little more if you need to thin out the batter)

1 teaspoon onion powder

Salt and pepper to taste

Olive oil for frying

INGREDIENTS FOR THE FRUITY SALSA:

½ cup mango, chopped

½ cup pineapple, chopped

½ a red onion, finely diced

¼ cup cilantro, finely chopped

Juice of 2 limes

½ teaspoon red pepper flakes, or to taste

DIRECTIONS:

The Tilapia

1. Preheat the oven to 375° F and place the tilapia fillets into an oven-safe dish. Squeeze ½ a lemon over each fillet and then sprinkle over with basil, garlic, and cilantro, then season the fish with salt and pepper to taste. Pop it into the oven for 15 minutes or until the fish flakes easily with a fork.

The Wraps

1. While the fish cooks, prepare the wraps. Mix all the ingredients for the wraps together in a bowl and allow to rest for 10 minutes. Heat up a non-stick skillet over a medium heat and add a little olive oil to grease the bottom of the pan (literally just a drop or 2; otherwise, the wraps will be very greasy). Add the wrap batter in $\frac{1}{3}$-cup scoops and swirl it around to coat the pan. Cook them for 2 minutes per side or until golden brown. Repeat until the batter is finished.

The Salsa and Assembly

1. Mix all the ingredients together in a bowl.
2. To assemble the wraps: Place the wrap on a plate. Load it up with the flaked tilapia and a generous helping of fruity salsa.

FRUITY LAMB KEBABS WITH A SPICY TWIST

Yields: 4 Servings

Perfect food for outdoor entertaining on a warm summer night!

INGREDIENTS FOR THE KEBABS:

1 pound leg of lamb, cut into cubes

⅛ pound free-range and nitrate-free bacon, cut into squares

1 onion, quartered

1 cup dried apricots, soaked overnight

2 onions, sliced thickly

4 tablespoons olive oil

4 tablespoons mild curry powder

4 garlic cloves, crushed

1 teaspoon turmeric

2 cups apple cider vinegar

1 cup smooth apricot jam, see recipe below

Zest and juice of 1 lemon

½ cup raw honey

INGREDIENTS FOR THE JAM:

12 apricots, pits removed and quartered

¼ cup raw honey

2 tablespoons lemon juice, freshly squeezed

1 packet gelatin

DIRECTIONS:

The Jam

1. Place the apricots into a saucepan and cook them over a medium heat, stirring often for about 20 minutes, then add the lemon juice and raw honey. By now all the big chunks should have broken down and your mixture should be more or less smooth. If you still have lumps, toss it into the blender and blitz it smooth, then add it back to the saucepan and continue.

2. Now is the tricky part. If you add the gelatin all at once, it will clump together in a gooey mess. What you need to do is sprinkle a tiny bit over the apricots when they are boiling rapidly (increase the heat if you need

to) and stir very quickly to ensure it gets absorbed evenly. Continue to do this until all the gelatin has been added—patience is the name of the game!

3. Once all the gelatin has been added, allow the jam to cook over a medium heat for a further 5 minutes. Remove from the heat and allow to cool slightly before decanting it into a jar and placing it into the fridge to cool completely.

The Kebabs

1. Thread the lamb cubes, bacon, quartered onion, and soaked apricots onto the skewers taking care to alternate the ingredients, then place the kebabs into a shallow dish.

2. Sauté the thickly sliced onion in the oil until it is softened but not browned, then add the curry powder, garlic, turmeric, vinegar, jam, lemon juice, lemon zest, and raw honey. Cook over a medium heat for 5 minutes and then remove the marinade from the heat and pour it over the kebabs. Cover them and place them in the fridge for at least 2 hours.

3. Preheat oven to 350° F.

4. Remove the kebabs from the marinade and place them on a grill over a baking tray in a single layer. Bake in the oven for about 25 minutes or until they are done. Alternatively, these are simply fantastic on the grill.

5. Pour the marinade into a saucepan and cook over a medium heat until the sauce begins to thicken.

6. Serve with a simple side salad and the dipping sauce.

SPICY CHICKEN THIGHS

Yields: 4 Servings

> **The perfect meal to eat while watching your favorite sport!**
> **Pairs incredibly well with a side of fruity slaw.**

INGREDIENTS:

12 bone-in chicken thighs, washed

¼ cup fresh thyme

¼ cup organic chicken stock

1 onion, diced

2 red chilies, chopped

1 green chili, chopped

1-inch piece of ginger, peeled and sliced

3 tablespoons ground allspice

2 tablespoons apple cider vinegar

2 tablespoons raw honey

½ teaspoon ground black pepper

Juice of 2 limes

¼ cup olive oil

DIRECTIONS:

1. Place the washed chicken into a large zippered plastic bag.
2. Place the remaining ingredients, except for the olive oil into the blender and process until smooth.
3. Now, with the blender still running, slowly add the olive oil until you have formed a smooth mixture.
4. Pour the marinade over the chicken pieces and seal the bag. Massage the bag to ensure that all the chicken pieces are covered with the marinade.

5. Pop the bag into the fridge for 4 hours so the chicken can really absorb the flavors.
6. Preheat the oven to 400° F and cover a baking tray with some foil. Set a grill rack on top and remove the chicken from the fridge.
7. Remove the chicken thighs from the marinade and lay them out on the grill rack. Discard the remaining marinade.
8. Place the chicken into the oven to grill for about 20 minutes or until cooked through. Turn the chicken pieces halfway through the cooking time to ensure even cooking.

SALADS

WARM BEEF TENDERLOIN SALAD

Yields: 2 Servings

> **The perfect salad to eat on its own or as a side to your favorite meal!**

INGREDIENTS FOR THE BEEF TENDERLOIN:

¼ cup ghee

2 4-ounce grass-fed beef tenderloin steaks

¼ cup coconut aminos

2 tablespoons freshly grated horseradish

INGREDIENTS FOR THE SALAD:

2 cups mixed salad greens

1 cup cherry tomatoes, halved

¼ cup red onion, thinly sliced

DIRECTIONS:

1. Preheat the oven to 350° F.
2. As the oven is preheating, melt the ghee in the oven in a glass dish big enough for both steaks.
3. Once the ghee is melted and bubbling, remove the dish from the oven and place both tenderloins in the dish.
4. Spoon the ghee over the steaks and gently pour the coconut aminos over the top.
5. Bake for 10 minutes, flip the tenderloins, and continue to cook for 20–35 minutes or until the internal temperature is 135° F, then remove them from the oven.
6. Spoon ½ a cup of the butter-coconut amino sauce from the pan into a separate bowl and mix with the horseradish, then spoon the sauce back over the tenderloins.

7. Allow the steaks to rest for 5 minutes while you assemble the salad.
8. Arrange the greens on 2 plates with the cherry tomatoes and the onions.
9. Slice your steaks into strips and place them on top of the salad.
10. Drizzle the horseradish sauce over the top.
11. Serve immediately.

MAHI MAHI SALSA SALAD

Yields: 2 Servings

INGREDIENTS:

2 mahi mahi fillets

¼ cup freshly squeezed lemon juice

1 mango, diced

1 avocado, diced

1 tomato, diced

¼ cup red onion, diced

3 tablespoons cilantro, chopped

Juice of 1 lime

¼ teaspoon cayenne pepper

Salt and pepper to taste

1 head of butter lettuce, chopped

Olive oil

DIRECTIONS:

1. Place the mahi mahi in a resealable plastic bag with ¼ cup of lemon juice and a dash of salt and pepper, and leave it in the refrigerator to marinate for 20 minutes.
2. In a bowl, combine the mango, avocado, tomato, red onion, cilantro, lime juice, and cayenne pepper, then season with salt and pepper and set aside.
3. Bring the grill to a medium-high heat.
4. Remove the mahi mahi from the plastic bag and brush the grill with a little olive oil to prevent the fish from sticking.
5. Grill for 3—4 minutes per side, until slightly opaque in the center. Allow to cool, then cut into bite-sized chunks.
6. Divide the lettuce onto 2 plates. Top with the salsa mixture and mahi mahi pieces.
7. Serve immediately.

BROCCOLI AND BACON SALAD

Yields: 2 Servings

INGREDIENTS FOR THE MAYONNAISE:

1 tablespoon apple cider vinegar

1 teaspoon salt

1 egg

1 cup olive oil

INGREDIENTS FOR THE SALAD:

¼ cup pumpkin seeds

6 strips of free-range and nitrate-free bacon

1 onion, diced

1 pound broccoli, cut into florets

½ cup raisins

½ cup Paleo mayonnaise

DIRECTIONS:

The Mayonnaise

1. Using your immersion blender in a narrow bowl, combine the vinegar, salt, and the egg, pulsing a few times until frothy.
2. Keep your blender running and add a few drops of oil at a time until an emulsion forms. Keep adding until all the oil is in and the mixture is the consistency of mayonnaise. Place into an airtight jar and refrigerate until chilled.

The Salad

1. Place the pumpkin seeds on a baking tray and toast them in a 350° F oven for about 10 minutes. Set aside to cool.
2. Fry the bacon in a nonstick skillet until it is crispy. Remove from the pan and when it is cool enough to handle, crumble it into pieces.

3. Use the bacon drippings to fry up your onions until they are golden and caramelized.
4. Combine the broccoli, bacon pieces, caramelized onion, raisins, and toasted pumpkin seeds in a salad bowl and toss to mix.
5. Add the chilled Paleo mayonnaise and toss again to ensure the whole salad is evenly coated.
6. Chill and serve.

POPEYE'S SALAD

Yields: 4 Servings

The tastiest way to get your greens in!

INGREDIENTS:

2 tablespoons olive oil

8 slices free-range and nitrate-free bacon, diced

1 onion, finely chopped

2 garlic cloves, finely chopped

½ cup organic beef stock

2 tablespoons apple cider vinegar

4 tablespoons maple syrup

4 cups baby spinach leaves

2 apples, peeled, cored, and diced

¼ cup dried cranberries

2 tablespoons walnuts, chopped

Salt and black pepper to taste

DIRECTIONS:

1. Heat up the olive oil in a saucepan over a medium heat and cook the bacon bits until they are crispy. Remove them from the pan with a slotted spoon and set aside.
2. Add the onion and garlic to the bacon drippings and cook over a medium heat until the onion is golden brown.
3. Now stir in the beef stock and bring it to a boil, then add the apple cider vinegar and maple syrup. Reduce the heat to low and allow the mixture to simmer for 5 minutes, then remove from the heat.
4. Divide the spinach leaves, apple, cranberries, and bacon evenly between 4 salad bowls.
5. Drizzle with the warm dressing from the pan and finish off with a sprinkle of chopped walnuts on top.
6. Season with salt and black pepper to taste and serve immediately.

ROAST CHICKEN AND ARUGULA SALAD

Yields: 4 Servings

This is a great recipe to use up leftover chicken!

INGREDIENTS FOR THE MAYONNAISE:

1 tablespoon apple cider vinegar

1 teaspoon salt

1 egg

1 cup olive oil

1 teaspoon dried mixed herbs

½ teaspoon crushed garlic

INGREDIENTS FOR THE SALAD:

4 roasted chicken breasts, diced

1 cup arugula, roughly chopped

1 cup seedless red grapes, cut in half

1 cup Paleo mayonnaise (recipe below)

½ cup roasted pecans, roughly chopped

1 red onion, very finely diced

Salt and black pepper to taste

DIRECTIONS:

The Mayonnaise

1. Using your immersion blender in a narrow bowl, combine the vinegar, salt, and the egg, pulsing a few times until frothy.

2. Keep your blender running and add a few drops of oil at a time until an emulsion forms. Keep adding until all the oil is in and the mixture is the consistency of mayonnaise. Place into an airtight jar and refrigerate until chilled.

3. Once chilled, stir in the crushed garlic and herbs until well combined. Set aside.

The Salad

1. Place all the ingredients into a large mixing bowl and toss to combine. Yes, it's that easy!

ISLAND-STYLE SALAD

Yields: 4 Servings

INGREDIENTS FOR THE SWEET CHILI SAUCE:

2 chargrilled red capsicum peppers (roast in a 450° F oven until blackened—keep an eye on them! Alternatively, grill them on the stove over a high heat)

1 red chili

¼ cup apple cider vinegar

¼ cup raw honey

⅛ cup water

1 tablespoon fish sauce (optional)

3 cloves garlic (you can roast these too, if you like)

1 teaspoon grated ginger

1 teaspoon arrowroot powder mixed with 2 teaspoons water

Juice of ½ lime

Salt and pepper to taste

INGREDIENTS FOR THE SALAD:

4 smoked chicken fillets, sliced

½ cup sweet chili sauce

1 large papaya, peeled, and cut into cubes

1 pineapple, peeled and cut into cubes

1 red pepper, cut into cubes

1 red onion, diced

3 tablespoons freshly chopped mint

3 tablespoons freshly chopped cilantro

DIRECTIONS:
Sweet Chili Sauce

1. Place all the ingredients except for the arrowroot mixture into the blender and whiz until smooth. Taste and adjust seasonings according to your taste preferences.
2. Pour the liquid into a saucepan and bring it to a boil over a medium-high heat, stirring frequently. Allow to cook for 5 minutes and then add the arrowroot mixture while stirring.

3. Once thickened, remove the sauce from the heat and allow to cool. Store in an airtight jar in the fridge until you are ready to use it.

The Salad

1. Place all the ingredients into a large salad bowl and toss to combine well. Serve chilled.

GRILLED ARTICHOKE AND PROSCIUTTO SALAD WITH ROASTED CHERRY TOMATOES

Yields: 2 Servings

INGREDIENTS:

2 cups cherry tomatoes

½ cup olive oil

1 jar artichokes

1 red onion, thinly sliced

1 celery stalk, thinly sliced

¼ cup balsamic vinegar

2 garlic cloves, minced

Juice and zest of 1 lemon

2 tablespoons fresh parsley, finely chopped

8 slices prosciutto, roughly chopped

¼ cup basil leaves, torn

salt and pepper to taste

DIRECTIONS:

1. Preheat the oven to 400°F.
2. Cut the cherry tomatoes in half and squeeze the flesh and juice out into a bowl and set aside. Place the shells onto a baking tray and drizzle with 2 tablespoons of the olive oil, season with salt and pepper, and pop them into the oven for 10–15 minutes. Remove and allow to cool.
3. Heat up another 2 tablespoons of the oil in a griddle pan over a high heat and grill the artichokes until they have dark brown stripes on them, then remove them from the heat and set them aside.
4. To the bowl with the tomato juice, add the onions, celery, balsamic vinegar, remaining olive oil, garlic, lemon zest, lemon juice, and chopped parsley, and stir together well.
5. Mix the artichokes, cherry tomatoes, and torn basil leaves together in a bowl and then pour the balsamic dressing mixture over them. Season with black pepper to taste and toss well to combine.
6. Lastly, add the prosciutto pieces and give it all one final mix.
7. Serve immediately and revel in the taste explosion in your mouth!

DINNER

ASIAN-STYLE PORK LETTUCE WRAPS

Yields: 2 servings

INGREDIENTS:

1 tablespoon olive oil

1 shallot, finely chopped

1-inch fresh ginger, peeled and grated

½ teaspoon crushed garlic

½ pound minced pork

1 tablespoon fish sauce

2 tablespoons coconut aminos

Juice and zest of 1 lime

2 tablespoons cilantro, chopped

2 head of gem lettuces, leaves separated (you can substitute any lettuce you like)

2 spring onions, chopped (these are optional, for garnish)

DIRECTIONS:

1. Heat up the olive oil in a heavy-bottomed skillet or wok until it is hot, then add the chopped shallots, grated ginger, and garlic, and cook for a couple of minutes.
2. Add the pork mince, fish sauce, coconut aminos, lime juice, and zest, and cook, stirring often until the meat is cooked through, then add the chopped cilantro and cook for another minute.
3. Remove from the heat and allow it to cool slightly.
4. To eat, spoon the mixture into the lettuce leaves, wrap them up into a bundle, and eat straightaway.

MEDITERRANEAN PIZZA A LA PALEO

Yields: 2—4 Servings

> **Enjoy pizza without feeling guilty!**

INGREDIENTS FOR THE CRUST:

2 cups shredded sweet potato

½ cup ground flaxseed

¼ cup almond flour

1 egg

1 tablespoon olive oil

1 tablespoon garlic powder

Salt and pepper to taste

INGREDIENTS FOR THE TOPPING:

½ cup cherry tomatoes, sliced thinly

¼ cup yellow zucchini, sliced thinly

¼ cup green zucchini, sliced thinly

¼ cup baby eggplant, sliced thinly

¼ cup black olives, sliced thinly

¼ cup red pepper, sliced thinly

Olive oil as needed

Fresh watercress leaves, for garnish

Balsamic vinegar, for drizzling

Salt and pepper to taste

DIRECTIONS:

1. Preheat the oven to 375° F and line a baking tray with parchment paper. Squeeze all the excess liquid out of the shredded sweet potato and add it to a bowl with the rest of the crust ingredients. Mix them together well until a ball of dough forms.

2. Shape the dough on the parchment-lined baking tray into a rectangle shape, using the dimensions of the tray as a guide. Try to get as even a layer as possible. You are aiming for about a ¼-inch thickness.

3. Place the crust in the oven and bake for 20 minutes.

4. Remove the crust and place another piece of parchment paper on top of it, and using another baking tray, flip the crust over and peel off the bottom piece of parchment paper.

5. Leaving the crust this side up, arrange the thinly sliced vegetables in layers, then brush the tops of them with some olive oil.
6. Season with a bit of salt and pepper and place the pizza back into the oven.
7. Bake for about 15 minutes or until the veggies are starting to brown.
8. Remove the pizza, garnish with the watercress leaves, and drizzle with some balsamic before serving.

ROASTED CORNISH GAME HENS WITH CARAMELIZED ONION RELISH

Yields: 4 Servings

INGREDIENTS FOR THE ONION RELISH:

2 tablespoons olive oil

2 pounds onions, cut into wedges

½ cup apple cider vinegar

½ cup raw honey

1 teaspoon mustard powder

2-cup glass jar with lid

INGREDIENTS FOR THE CORNISH HENS:

1 teaspoon ground sage

½ teaspoon ground thyme

½ teaspoon ground marjoram

½ teaspoon ground rosemary

½ teaspoon ground nutmeg

1 tablespoon dried basil

2 tablespoons lemon pepper

1 tablespoon salt

4 Cornish game hens, approximately 1½ pounds each

2 tablespoons olive oil

1 onion, diced

1 green pepper, diced

2 stalks celery, diced

DIRECTIONS:

The Onions

1. Heat up the olive oil over a low heat in a deep frying pan. Add the onions and cook, stirring occasionally, for 30 minutes until they are softened and beginning to brown.

2. Add the vinegar, raw honey, and mustard to the pan and increase the heat to medium-low. Cook for 20 minutes, stirring occasionally, until the relish starts to thicken and the liquid has evaporated. Add salt and pepper to taste.

3. Transfer the relish into the glass jar and seal it. Place in the refrigerator. Use within 3 months. Once opened, keep refrigerated and use within 2 weeks.

The Cornish Hens

1. Preheat your oven to 375° F.
2. Mix the sage, thyme, marjoram, rosemary, nutmeg, basil, lemon-pepper, and salt together in a small bowl. Rub the hens with the olive oil and then season them with the mixture you made.
3. Place the hens on 2 baking trays, 2 per tray, making sure that they have plenty of space. Stuff the cavities of each of the hens loosely with the diced onion, green pepper, and celery.
4. Roast the hens for 60 minutes. The hens are done when the juices run clear and the internal temperature reaches 175° F. Remove from the oven and tent with foil to rest for 10 minutes.
5. Carve and serve with some caramelized onion relish.

MUSSELS POT WITH
A CRUSTY PALEO BAGUETTE

Yields: 4 Servings

> **Comfort food at its finest!**

INGREDIENTS FOR THE MUSSELS:

3 onions, diced

8 cloves garlic, minced

2 pounds tomatoes, diced

½ cup tomato paste

¼ cup olive oil

3 red chilies, chopped and seeds removed

1 cup water

2 tablespoons oregano

2 tablespoons basil

2 tablespoons parsley

Salt and black pepper to taste

3 pounds mussels

INGREDIENTS FOR THE PALEO BAGUETTE:

2 cups almond flour

¼ cup finely ground flax seeds

2 tablespoons organic gluten-free baking powder

1 teaspoon salt

1 teaspoon thyme

1 teaspoon garlic powder

3 eggs, beaten

3 tablespoons organic apple cider vinegar

2 tablespoons raw honey

½–1 cup boiling water

Olive oil as needed

DIRECTIONS:

The Mussels

1. Heat the olive oil in a large skillet over a medium heat. Sauté the onions and garlic until they begin to brown, then scrape the mixture into a slow cooker.
2. Add the rest of the ingredients, except for the mussels, and cook on high for 3 hours.
3. Now add the mussels, cover, and cook on high for a further 30 minutes.

The Baguette

1. Preheat the oven to 350° F and line a French bread pan with some parchment paper. Mix the dry ingredients together in a bowl. Mix the wet ingredients (not the boiling water) together in a separate bowl.
2. Pour the wet bowl into the dry bowl and mix, then slowly add the boiling water. Add enough that the dough comes together but is not too sticky to work with.
3. Shape the dough into a baguette and place it into the pan. Pour a little olive oil onto your hands and smooth out the top of the dough. This also allows a delicious golden crunchy crust to form when the bread bakes. Bake for 1 hour, then allow to cool on a rack.
4. To serve: Ladle the mussels into a bowl with plenty of tomato sauce and serve with the crusty baguette and a mixed green salad on the side.

PERFECT PALEO PAELLA

Yields: 4 Servings

INGREDIENTS:

4 cups cauliflower, cut into florets

2½ cups chicken broth

2 tablespoons olive oil

8 ounces chorizo sausage, casings removed and crumbled

1 onion, chopped

2 tomatoes, chopped

1 red pepper, diced

4 garlic cloves, minced

1 teaspoon saffron threads

½ teaspoon smoked paprika

2 tablespoons fish sauce

8 mussels, scrubbed clean

8 clams, scrubbed clean

1 pound shrimp, peeled and deveined

Salt and black pepper to taste

2 lemons, cut into wedges, for serving

Freshly chopped parsley for garnish

DIRECTIONS:

1. Add the cauliflower to your blender and blend until it resembles rice. Set aside for later.

2. Place the chicken broth into a saucepan and gently heat it up over a medium heat.

3. In a separate, large skillet, heat half the olive oil and brown the chorizo over a medium heat, then add the rest of the olive oil, onions, tomatoes, red pepper, garlic, saffron, paprika, and fish sauce and cook until the onions are soft and translucent.

4. Pour 1 cup of the warmed chicken broth into the skillet and use a wooden spoon to scrape off any browned bits that have stuck to the bottom of the pan.

5. Add the cauliflower rice and allow to simmer gently for about 15 minutes. Take care to keep the heat low; if it is too high the cauliflower will overcook.

6. Bring the rest of the chicken broth to a boil over a medium-high heat, and add the clams and mussels. Cover the pan and cook for 10 minutes or until the shells have opened up. When they are done, remove them from the broth with a slotted spoon and set aside, discarding any that have not opened.

7. Now add the shrimp to the broth in two batches. Allow them to cook for about 5 minutes, or until they are pink, then remove them with the slotted spoon and set them aside with the clams and mussels.

8. Once the cauliflower has cooked and the liquid in the pan has reduced, place the clams, mussels, and shrimp into the cauliflower rice and gently toss to mix them in.

9. Allow to cook for another 10 minutes and then remove the pan from the heat.

10. Leave it for a further 10 minutes before serving it with a sprinkling of freshly chopped parsley and some lemon wedges.

CIDER-GLAZED QUAIL WITH APPLE AND SAUSAGE STUFFING

Yields: 4 Servings

This meal is sure to impress your friends!

INGREDIENTS:

4 whole quail

1 tablespoon olive oil

1 onion, finely chopped

6 ounces Italian sausage meat

1 apple, finely chopped

¼ cup pecans, finely chopped

1 teaspoon thyme

1 tablespoon raw honey

½ cup apple cider

1 tablespoon ghee

Salt and pepper to taste

DIRECTIONS:

1. Rinse the quail and pat them dry.
2. Heat up the olive oil in a skillet over a medium heat, add the onion, and cook until translucent.
3. Add the sausage meat, breaking it up with a wooden spoon until it is all crumbled, and cook until browned.
4. Add the thyme, pecans, and apple. Stir thoroughly to combine and leave it to cook for 5 minutes.
5. Remove the stuffing from heat and set it aside to cool.
6. Whisk the raw honey and the apple cider together in a saucepan over a medium-high heat.
7. Bring the raw honey and cider mixture to a boil, then reduce the heat to a simmer. In 5 to 10 minutes, the glaze should reduce by half. At this point, remove the pan from heat and add the ghee, whisking to combine it well.

8. Season each bird with salt and pepper. Gently stuff each bird with your stuffing mix, but don't pack it in too tight—you should only use about half the stuffing.

9. Brush each quail with the glaze and place them on a baking tray. Put them in a preheated oven set at 350° F for 25 minutes.

10. Remove the quail from the oven. Now set your oven to broil, glaze the birds for a second time, and place them under the broiler for 2–3 minutes. This will crisp up the outside and caramelize the glaze. Remove from the broiler and glaze them one more time.

11. Serve the quail on a bed of the leftover stuffing with a side of your choice—simple and elegant!

AROMATIC VEGGIE POT

Yields: 4 Servings

INGREDIENTS:

2 tablespoons olive oil

2 cups button mushrooms, sliced

1 onion, sliced

1 red pepper, sliced

4 garlic cloves, crushed

½ pound butternut squash, cut into cubes

1 teaspoon cumin

½ teaspoon ground ginger

½ teaspoon ground cinnamon

Ground black pepper to taste

¼ pound tomatoes, peeled and roughly chopped

½ cup organic vegetable stock

2 tablespoons tomato paste

Freshly chopped cilantro for garnish

DIRECTIONS:

1. Heat up 1 tablespoon of olive oil in a large pot over a medium heat and then add the mushrooms. Sauté them until they are soft and just beginning to brown, then remove them from the pot and set them aside.

2. Add the other tablespoon of oil to the pot and then toss in the onions, garlic, and red pepper and cook until the vegetables are soft—about 10 minutes.

3. Add the butternut cubes and allow them to cook for a further 5 minutes, stirring frequently to prevent them from sticking.

4. Add all the spices to the pot and stir well to combine. Allow them to cook for 1 minute until aromatic.

5. Add the tomatoes and cook for 5 minutes, then add the tomato paste and stock and stir well to combine.

6. Put the lid on the pot at an angle and allow the pot to simmer over a medium to low heat for about 25 minutes, or until the butternut is soft. Stir occasionally, but take care to be gentle so you don't turn the butternut to mush.

7. Once the butternut is soft, stir in the mushrooms, leave the lid off, and allow them to heat through for about 5 minutes.
8. Season with some black pepper to taste.
9. Serve hot on a bed of cauliflower rice or couscous with some freshly chopped cilantro sprinkled on top.

BRAISED EISBEIN

Yields: 4 Servings

INGREDIENTS:

1 pound Eisbein (pork shank cut, bone in)

4 whole cloves

2 bay leaves

2-inch knob of ginger, peeled and chopped

1 bunch spring onions, ends trimmed and peeled

2 tablespoons olive oil

2 cups water

¼ cup coconut aminos

¼ cup balsamic vinegar

2 garlic cloves, crushed

2 tablespoons raw honey

1 tablespoon fish sauce

1 teaspoon arrowroot powder mixed with 1 teaspoon water

1 tablespoon sesame oil

DIRECTIONS:

1. Place the pork in a pot with the cloves, bay leaves, half the chopped ginger, and half the spring onions. Cover the meat with water and bring the pot to a boil over a medium heat.
2. Reduce the heat and cook for 2 hours until tender. Remove from the pot and set aside. Discard the water.
3. Heat up the olive oil in a deep saucepan and sauté the remaining spring onions, garlic, and ginger.
4. Add the water, coconut aminos, balsamic vinegar, raw honey, and fish sauce and cook on a low heat until bubbling.
5. Add the pork to the sauce and cook for 10 minutes, turning after 5 minutes if necessary to coat the entire piece of meat. Remove the meat to a serving plate to rest.
6. Add the arrowroot mixture to the sauce and stir until thickened.
7. Lastly, stir in the sesame oil and pour the sauce over the Eisbein on the serving plate.
8. Serve with the sides of your choice.

PISTACHIO PORK

Yields: 4 Servings

> **Something different to make for a special occasion!**
> **Delicious served with sweet potato wedges.**

INGREDIENTS:

½ cup almond flour

1 cup Paleo bread crumbs (simply place Paleo bread in the food processor and whiz it up—best not to use very fresh bread)

2 tablespoons mustard powder

¾ cup pistachio nuts, finely chopped

2 eggs, beaten

8 pork fillet medallions, trimmed of any excess fat

Olive oil as needed

DIRECTIONS:

1. Place the flour on a plate.
2. On a second plate, combine the bread crumbs, mustard powder, and pistachio nuts.
3. Place the eggs in a bowl.
4. Flatten the pork fillets with a meat mallet until they are nice and thin.
5. Turn each pork fillet in the flour, then the egg, then the bread crumb mix. Continue until all the pork fillets have been coated.
6. Heat up a generous amount of olive oil in a skillet over a medium heat and gently fry the coated pork fillets until they are all golden brown and crispy.

SWEET AND SPICY CHICKEN AND PRAWN CURRY

Yields: 4 Servings

INGREDIENTS:

½ pound chicken breasts, cubed

1 cup crushed canned tomatoes

4 tablespoons olive oil, plus more for frying

2 tablespoons crushed garlic

1 tablespoon turmeric

1 tablespoon cumin

2 tablespoons curry powder

½ pound prawns, peeled and deveined

1 tablespoon ghee

2 cups grated onion

1 tablespoon curry paste

1-inch knob of ginger, peeled and grated

4 tablespoons raw honey

¼ teaspoon saffron

1 can apricot halves, drained

1 can coconut milk

1 cup coconut cream

1 teaspoon cayenne pepper (or to taste)

Salt and pepper to taste

1 bunch cilantro, roughly chopped

DIRECTIONS:

1. Place the chicken pieces into a zippered plastic bag with the tomatoes, oil, garlic, cumin, turmeric, cayenne pepper, and curry powder for at least an hour.

2. Remove the chicken pieces from the marinade and set aside, then add the prawns to the bag and marinade them for at least an hour.

3. Heat up a little oil in a large saucepan and cook the chicken pieces until they are done—about 10–15 minutes. Take care to turn them often to ensure even cooking.

4. Now do the same with the prawns, but only cook them for about 5 minutes.

5. Place the chicken and prawns on a plate, cover them, and keep them warm while you complete the rest of the recipe.

6. In the same pan, melt the ghee and sauté the onion until soft, then add curry paste, ginger, raw honey, saffron, apricots, coconut milk, and coconut cream. Allow the sauce to simmer over a medium heat until it starts to thicken.
7. Once thickened, stir in the tomato marinade and simmer for a further 10 minutes until bubbly.
8. Now add the chicken and prawns back to the pan and allow them to heat through.
9. Serve on a bed of cauliflower rice with some sambals and a generous garnish of cilantro.

EASY ROAST CHICKEN WITH BACON STUFFING

Yields: 4 Servings

Serve with your favorite side dishes!

INGREDIENTS:

1 tablespoon olive oil, plus more for drizzling

1 cup mushrooms, finely chopped

1 leek, finely chopped

2 garlic cloves, crushed

8 free-range and nitrate-free bacon slices, finely chopped

1 cup Paleo breadcrumbs

2 tablespoons freshly chopped thyme

1 egg, beaten

1 whole chicken, washed and patted dry

Salt and black pepper to taste

DIRECTIONS:

1. Preheat the oven to 350° F and line a baking tray with foil.
2. Heat the olive oil in a skillet over a medium-high heat, then add the mushrooms, leeks, garlic, and bacon, and cook until the bacon and mushrooms are golden brown.
3. Transfer the mixture to a bowl and allow it to cool slightly, then mix in the breadcrumbs, half the thyme, and beaten egg. Mix together thoroughly.
4. Loosely stuff the cavity of the chicken with the bacon mixture and place the bird on the baking tray.
5. Drizzle the outside of the chicken with olive oil and season with salt and pepper. Sprinkle the remainder of the thyme over the top and pop it in the oven for 90 minutes or until succulent and brown. (The chicken is cooked when the juices run clear.)
6. Slice, serve with your favorite sides, and enjoy!

SIMPLE SALMON STEAK

Yields: 4 Servings

INGREDIENTS:

¼ cup olive oil

1 onion, finely chopped

¼ cup organic chicken stock

Zest and juice of 2 lemons

4 salmon steaks

½ pound sweet potato, peeled and cut into chunks

1 head of garlic, cut in half horizontally

Black pepper to taste

4 cups baby spinach leaves

1 bunch of asparagus, ends trimmed

DIRECTIONS:

1. Preheat the oven to 400° F.
2. Add half the oil to a skillet and heat it over a medium heat, then add the onion and sauté until the onion is soft but not brown. Now add the chicken stock and stir together well. Allow to cook for 5 minutes until the stock is hot.
3. Remove from the heat and allow to cool for 5 minutes, then stir in the lemon zest and juice.
4. Place the salmon steaks into the mixture to marinate for 30 minutes.
5. Place the potatoes and garlic onto a baking tray that has been lightly greased, and drizzle the remaining olive oil over it.
6. Place into the oven to roast for 15 minutes.
7. Remove the salmon from the marinade and place it onto a separate baking tray. Season the steaks with some black pepper.
8. Add the spinach and asparagus to the potatoes and pour over the marinade liquid. Stir to ensure that the vegetables are well coated.
9. Place the steaks into the oven with the vegetables and allow them to cook for about 10 minutes depending on the thickness of the steaks. The salmon is done when it flakes easily with a fork.

10. When the vegetables are tender, remove the tray from the oven, squeeze the roasted garlic cloves over them, and stir well.

11. Serve immediately and devour!

FRAGRANT AND FRUITY LAMB STEW

Yields: 4 Servings

INGREDIENTS:

1 pound lamb knuckles

3 tablespoons olive oil

2 tablespoons ghee

2 onions, finely chopped

4 carrots, peeled and sliced

4 garlic cloves, crushed

1 teaspoon cumin

1 teaspoon cinnamon

1 teaspoon ginger

1 teaspoon cilantro

1 teaspoon paprika

1 cup dried apricots

1 cup balsamic vinegar

1 cup water

Salt and pepper to taste

DIRECTIONS:

1. Season the lamb knuckles with salt and pepper.
2. Heat up the oil and ghee in a large skillet, and fry the lamb knuckles in batches until they are golden brown on all sides. Set aside.
3. Now add the onion, carrots, and garlic to the pan and cook until they are tender.
4. Place the browned meat back into the pan and add all the spices. Stir well and allow to cook for a minute or 2 until deliciously fragrant.
5. Now add the balsamic vinegar, water, and dried apricots and give it all a good stir.
6. Cover the pot with a lid and allow to cook over a low heat for about 90 minutes or until the meat is falling off the bone.
7. Serve with some cauliflower rice tossed with freshly chopped herbs.

PEPPER BEEF STEW

Yields: 4 Servings

> **This is a great stand-alone dish, but you can serve it
> with cauliflower rice as well.**

INGREDIENTS:

3 tablespoons olive oil

1 pound stewing steak, cubed

2 onions, chopped

4 garlic cloves, crushed

2 red peppers, chopped

2 tablespoons paprika

1 tablespoon dried mixed
   herbs

¼ pound sweet potato, cubed

2 carrots, sliced

1 tablespoon arrowroot powder
   mixed with 1 tablespoon water

1 cup water

2 cups organic beef stock

½ cup coconut cream

¼ pound tomatoes, chopped

DIRECTIONS:

1. Heat up the oil in a large stew pot and fry the steak cubes in batches until they are brown. Set aside.
2. Add the onions and garlic to the same pot and cook until they are soft, then add the red peppers and sauté for a further 5 minutes until they too have softened.
3. Add the paprika and mixed herbs and stir.
4. Put the steak back into the pot along with the potatoes, carrots, water, and stock, and allow to simmer over a low heat for an hour or until the potatoes and carrots are tender.
5. Now stir in the arrowroot mixture and allow to simmer and thicken.
6. Once thickened, remove from the heat and stir through the coconut cream.

CURRIED FISH FILLETS

Yields: 4 Servings

INGREDIENTS:

1 tablespoon olive oil

1 onion, chopped

1 teaspoon grated ginger

1 teaspoon turmeric

1 tablespoon freshly chopped cilantro

1 tablespoon curry powder

¾ cup water

¾ cup coconut milk

½ cup tomato paste

½ pound skinless hake fillets

Salt and pepper to taste

DIRECTIONS:

1. Preheat oven to 350° F.
2. Heat the oil in a skillet over a medium heat and sauté the onion until soft, then add the ginger, turmeric, cilantro, and curry powder, and continue to cook for 1 minute, stirring constantly.
3. Add the water and coconut milk to the pan and allow to heat through, then stir in the tomato paste and allow to simmer until it starts to thicken.
4. Place the hake fillets into a casserole dish and season them with salt and pepper.
5. Pour the sauce over the hake fillets, ensuring they are all coated, and bake for 30 minutes or until the fish flakes easily with a fork.
6. Serve hot on a bed of cauliflower rice with chopped cilantro garnish.

SIDES

BAKED SWEET POTATOES

Yields: 4 Servings

INGREDIENTS:

4 sweet potatoes, washed and dried

1 large, ripe avocado

½ teaspoon crushed garlic

1 teaspoon lemon juice

¼ pound free-range and nitrate-free bacon, diced and cooked until crispy

4 tablespoons chives, chopped

Salt and black pepper to taste

DIRECTIONS:

1. Preheat the oven to 400° F.
2. Wrap each sweet potato individually in foil and bake for 30 minutes in the preheated oven. Then open the foil and bake for a further 10–15 minutes until the potatoes are cooked through, then remove from the oven and allow them to cool slightly while you prepare the topping.
3. Mash the avocado with the garlic and lemon juice and add salt and black pepper to taste.
4. Add the bacon bits and chives and stir together well.
5. Cut a cross in the top of each sweet potato and gently squeeze the sides.
6. Spoon ¼ of the avocado mixture on top of each sweet potato and serve immediately.

HERBED PARSNIP AND TURNIP PURÉE

Yields: 4 Servings

This dish is a fantastic accompaniment to roast meat.

INGREDIENTS:

1 pound parsnips, peeled and cut into chunks

½ pound turnips, peeled and cut into chunks

2 cloves garlic, minced

½ bunch of fresh thyme

3½ cups coconut milk

½ cup ghee, cut into cubes

Salt and freshly ground black pepper to taste

DIRECTIONS:

1. Add the parsnips, turnips, garlic, thyme, and the coconut milk to a medium saucepan. Set the heat to medium and cover with the lid at an angle.
2. Slowly bring to a simmer and leave it for 25 minutes or until tender. The tip of a knife should easily go through both the parsnips and turnips.
3. Remove the pot from heat and drain the liquids into a measuring jug. Remove the thyme, leaving the parsnips and turnips in the pot.
4. Add the ghee and about 1 cup of the cooking liquid, then season with the ground black pepper and salt. Using your immersion blender, blend until smooth, adding more cooking liquids as required.

VEGGIE CHIPS

Yields: 4 Servings

A healthy alternative to fat-laden chips! A mandoline would be great to use for cutting the veggies here.

INGREDIENTS:

2 sweet potatoes, thinly sliced

2 carrots, thinly sliced

2 zucchini, thinly sliced

Macadamia oil for frying

Salt to taste

DIRECTIONS:

1. Heat up the macadamia oil in a heavy-bottomed frying pan. The oil should be about ½-inch deep. Test to see if it is hot enough by carefully dropping in a veggie slice. When it sizzles, the oil is ready.

2. Gently add the assorted vegetables, taking care not to overcrowd the pan, as they will all stick together. Cook in two batches if necessary. Deep fry until the veggies are crisp; this should take about 10 minutes.

3. Remove with a slotted spoon, sprinkle with salt, and leave to drain on paper towels.

CARAMELIZED BRUSSELS SPROUTS AND ONIONS

Yields: 4 Servings

> **Serve with mains of your choice, though this side goes especially well with pork!**

INGREDIENTS:

1 pound Brussels sprouts

2 onions, peeled and sliced

¼ cup freshly squeezed orange juice

¼ cup olive oil

2 teaspoons stone-ground mustard (or mustard powder)

2 teaspoons apple cider vinegar

2 teaspoons maple syrup

½ teaspoon salt

2 teaspoons bacon grease (or substitute ghee)

DIRECTIONS:

1. Cut off the base of the Brussels sprouts (just the white part—if you cut too high the leaves will fall apart). Now cut them in half down the middle and set aside with the sliced onions.

2. Add the rest of the ingredients, except for the bacon grease, to your food processor, and puree until smooth. Set aside.

3. Set a large saucepan over a medium-high heat, then add the bacon grease, the onion slices, and the Brussels sprouts to the pan. Take care to keep the cut side of the sprouts facing down as you gently move them around the pan.

4. After 5 minutes, the sprouts should be nicely brown on the cut side, and the onions translucent. Now pour the sauce from the food processor over the onions and sprouts into the hot pan. It should sizzle like crazy!
5. Shake the handle of the pan a little to move the sprouts and the onions around as they can easily burn. Remove from heat as soon as the desired amount of caramelizing has occurred.

HERB FOCACCIA

Yields: 4 Servings

You won't want to stop at one slice!

INGREDIENTS:

2 teaspoons salt

1 tablespoon water

3 tablespoons olive oil

1½ cups almond flour

½ cup arrowroot powder

2 tablespoons garlic powder

2 tablespoons dried oregano

1 teaspoon baking soda

1 tablespoon apple cider vinegar

2 eggs

DIRECTIONS:

1. Preheat the oven to 400°F.
2. Grease a baking tray or cover it with parchment paper.
3. Stir together 1 teaspoon salt, 1 tablespoon water, and 1½ tablespoons olive oil in a small bowl and set it aside.
4. Mix together the almond flour, arrowroot powder, garlic, oregano, remaining salt, and the baking soda in a medium mixing bowl.
5. Now add the remaining olive oil, apple cider vinegar, and eggs, and mix until a dough ball forms.
6. Place the dough in the baking tray and spread it out in an even layer, about ¼- to ½-inch thick.
7. Now pour the salt, olive oil, and water mixture over the top and rub it in.
8. Bake for 20 minutes or until nicely golden on top.

FRUITY SLAW

Yields: 4 Servings

INGREDIENTS FOR THE FRUITY SLAW:

3 tablespoons red onion, finely chopped

¼ cup raisins

⅓ cup toasted walnuts, coarsely chopped

½ cup carrots, shredded

2 cups cabbage, shredded

2 teaspoons lemon juice

2 tablespoons raw honey

½ cup Paleo mayonnaise

1 apple, cored and chopped

½ cup pineapple, chopped

¼ teaspoon salt

¼ teaspoon pepper

INGREDIENTS FOR THE MAYONNAISE:

1 tablespoon apple cider vinegar

1 teaspoon salt

1 egg

1 cup olive oil

DIRECTIONS:

The Mayonnaise

1. Using your immersion blender in a narrow bowl, combine the vinegar, salt, and egg. Pulse a few times until frothy.

2. Keep your blender running and add a few drops of oil at a time until an emulsion forms. Keep adding until all the oil is in and the mixture is the consistency of mayonnaise.

The Slaw

1. Toss the onion, raisins, walnuts, carrots, and cabbage in a large salad bowl.

2. Combine the salt and pepper, lemon juice, raw honey, and mayonnaise in a small mixing bowl, pour it over the cabbage mixture, and toss it thoroughly to coat.

3. Fold in the chopped apple and pineapple, cover, and then refrigerate until ready to serve.

LEMON AND GARLIC ASPARAGUS

Yields: 4 Servings

Simple and elegant!

INGREDIENTS:

2 teaspoons olive oil

1 pound asparagus, trimmed

2 garlic cloves, minced

1 teaspoon fresh lemon juice

¼ teaspoon ground black pepper

¼ teaspoon salt

DIRECTIONS:

1. Heat a large, heavy pan with the olive oil over a medium-high heat; swirl the pan to ensure an even coat. Sauté the asparagus for 3 minutes or until they are tender.
2. Now add the garlic and cook for a further minute, stirring regularly.
3. Remove from the heat and season with salt, pepper, and lemon juice, tossing to coat.

CARAMELIZED CARROTS

Yields: 4 Servings

It doesn't get easier than this!

INGREDIENTS:

2 pounds carrots, peeled and cut into sticks

¼ cup ghee

¼ cup maple syrup or raw honey

¼ teaspoon salt

¼ teaspoon pepper

DIRECTIONS:

1. Boil the carrots in a saucepan for 8 to 10 minutes until tender. Transfer to a bowl.

2. Melt the ghee in the same saucepan over a medium heat and stir in the remaining ingredients. Once the ingredients are mixed and dissolved into the ghee, re-introduce the carrots to the saucepan. Cook for 5 minutes, mixing continuously.

HERBED CAULIFLOWER MASH

Yields: 4 Servings

INGREDIENTS:

2 pounds cauliflower, trimmed and cut into florets

4 tablespoons ghee

1 tablespoon sage

1 tablespoon garlic, minced

Salt and pepper to taste

DIRECTIONS:

1. Bring a pot of water to boil over a high heat. Add the cauliflower and cook for 15 minutes, until the cauliflower is tender.
2. Drain the cauliflower and return it to the pot on low heat, adding the ghee.
3. Mash the tender cauliflower together with the ghee, then add the garlic and sage, mixing well. Serve with any dinner!

SPICY ROASTED VEGGIE CHIPS

Yields: 2—4 Servings

INGREDIENTS:

1 sweet potato, peeled and thinly sliced

2 carrots, peeled and thinly sliced

¼ pound butternut squash, peeled and thinly sliced

¼ cup olive oil

1 teaspoon chili powder—or to taste

1 teaspoon garlic powder

1 teaspoon onion powder

½ teaspoon salt

DIRECTIONS:

1. Preheat the oven to 400° F, and line two baking sheets with parchment paper.
2. Mix the veggie slices with the olive oil and spices, and toss to ensure they are evenly coated.
3. Lay the slices out on the parchment-lined baking trays and bake for 30 minutes or until they are golden brown and crispy.
4. Turn the chips at least twice during cooking time to ensure even cooking.

SAVORY SWEET POTATO SALAD WITH GARLIC AND MUSTARD MAYO

Yields: 4 Servings

INGREDIENTS FOR THE SALAD:

1 pound sweet potato, peeled and cut into chunks

½ cup Paleo mayonnaise, recipe below

1 red pepper, finely chopped

6 spring onions, finely sliced

2 gherkins, finely chopped

¼ cup chives, chopped

Salt and black pepper to taste

INGREDIENTS FOR THE MAYONNAISE:

1 tablespoon apple cider vinegar

1 teaspoon garlic salt

1 egg

1 cup olive oil

2 tablespoons Dijon mustard

DIRECTIONS:

The Mayonnaise

1. Using your immersion blender in a narrow bowl, combine the vinegar, garlic salt, and the egg. Pulse a few times until frothy.
2. Keep your blender running and add a few drops of oil at a time until an emulsion forms. Keep adding until all the oil is in and the mixture is the consistency of mayonnaise.
3. Gently stir in the mustard, and place it in the fridge to chill while you prepare the salad.

The Salad

1. Bring a pot of salted water to a boil and add the sweet potato chunks. Cook until they are tender. Take care not to overcook them as the salad will be mushy. Once they are done, drain the water off and allow them to cool down slightly before mixing them with the rest of the ingredients.
2. Toss gently to combine everything and serve warm or chilled.

DUCHESS POTATOES

Yields: 6 Servings

INGREDIENTS:

2 pounds sweet potatoes, peeled and
   cubed

¼ cup coconut cream

¼ cup ghee

3 egg yolks

2 tablespoons freshly chopped parsley

1 tablespoon onion powder

Melted ghee for brushing

DIRECTIONS:

1. Preheat the oven to 400° F and line a baking tray with parchment paper.
2. Place the cubed potatoes into a pot of water and bring them to a boil. Allow them to cook for about 15 minutes or until they are tender, then drain them and return them to the pot.
3. Add the coconut cream to the pot and use a hand-held beater to whisk them until they are smooth, then stir in the ghee and egg yolks.
4. Add the onion powder and parsley and mix well.
5. Place the mixture into a piping bag with a large star nozzle attached, and pipe swirls onto the parchment paper (or you could simply dollop spoonfuls of the mixture onto the pan, like you would for a cookie).
6. Brush the tops gently with some melted ghee and then pop them into the oven for 20 minutes or until they are golden brown and the edges are crispy.

*Chefs tip—sprinkle a dusting of paprika on top for something different or add curry powder to the potato mixture. Have fun experimenting—the possibilities are endless!

VEGGIE STACKS

Yields: 6 Servings

INGREDIENTS:

1 butternut squash, peeled and sliced

4 sweet potatoes, peeled and sliced

2 onions, peeled and sliced

¼ cup ghee, melted

¼ cup freshly chopped herbs of your choice

1 teaspoon garlic powder

1 teaspoon red pepper flakes

DIRECTIONS:

1. Preheat oven to 350° F.
2. Place the squash, potato, and onion slices into a big bowl and drizzle the melted ghee over them. Add the herbs, garlic powder, and red pepper flakes, and toss well to combine.
3. Use a piece of foil to assemble each of the 6 stacks. Build the vegetable stacks, alternating between the squash, potato, and onion, until all the ingredients have been used up.
4. Pour over any leftover ghee and scrape all the spices onto the stacks.
5. Wrap the foil parcels up and bake for about 30 minutes or until the veggies are tender.
6. Take care when unwrapping the stacks, as the steam inside is hot and will burn you.
7. Serve immediately.

SPICY POTATO SALAD

Yields: 4—6 Servings

INGREDIENTS FOR THE SALAD:

1 pound sweet potatoes, peeled and cut into bite-sized cubes

2 tablespoons olive oil

2 onions, diced

2 tablespoons curry powder

1 cup Paleo mayonnaise, recipe below

¼ cup freshly chopped parsley

3 eggs, boiled, peeled, and roughly chopped

INGREDIENTS FOR THE MAYONNAISE:

1 tablespoon apple cider vinegar

1 teaspoon salt

1 egg

1 cup olive oil

DIRECTIONS:

The Mayonnaise

1. Using your immersion blender in a narrow bowl, combine the vinegar, salt, and the egg. Pulse a few times until frothy.
2. Keep your blender running and add a few drops of oil at a time until an emulsion forms. Keep adding until all the oil is in and the mixture is the consistency of mayonnaise.

The Salad

1. Boil the potato cubes in a pot of salted water until they are just tender, then drain them and allow them to cool down.
2. Heat up the olive oil in a nonstick skillet and sauté the onions until they are soft, then add the curry powder and cook for 2 minutes until fragrant.
3. Remove the onions from the heat and allow them to cool down, then stir them into the mayonnaise, along with the chopped parsley.
4. Place the potatoes and eggs into a big bowl and pour the mayonnaise over them. Toss gently to ensure the potatoes are well coated.

RAVISHING RATATOUILLE

Yields: 4 Servings

INGREDIENTS:

3 tablespoons olive oil

1 onion, diced

2 garlic cloves, minced

1 red pepper, cubed

1 yellow pepper, cubed

1 eggplant, cubed

¼ cup organic vegetable stock

3 pounds tomatoes, cubed

4 zucchini, cubed

1 tablespoon fresh thyme

Salt and black pepper to taste

DIRECTIONS:

1. Heat the oil in a nonstick skillet and sauté the onions and garlic until they are soft, then add the peppers and cook for 5 minutes.

2. Add the eggplant and fry for 2 minutes, then pour in the vegetable stock. Reduce the heat and allow to simmer for 10 minutes.

3. Add the tomatoes and cook for a further 5 minutes.

4. Lastly, add the zucchini and thyme and stir to combine. Season with salt and pepper and cook until the zucchini is soft.

5. Serve immediately with the mains of your choice.

DESSERTS

SIMPLY AMAZING CHOCOLATE MOUSSE

Yields: 4 Servings

> **A decadent and healthy way to enjoy chocolate!**

INGREDIENTS:

1 ripe avocado

6 dates, pitted

1 cup coconut milk

½ cup cacao powder, plus extra for dusting

3 tablespoons raw honey

1 tablespoon vanilla extract

1 teaspoon instant coffee (optional)

¼ teaspoon salt

Fresh mint and raspberries, for garnish

DIRECTIONS:

1. Place all the ingredients into your blender and process until smooth and well-combined. Scrape down the sides regularly to make sure everything gets mixed in.
2. Transfer the mixture to a bowl, and then, using your hand-held mixer, beat the mixture until light and fluffy.
3. Divide the mixture into 4 ramekins, top with a sprig of fresh mint and a couple of raspberries (optional), and place them in the fridge to chill for 6 hours.

CAKE IN A SKILLET

Yields: 4—6 Servings

> **Just in case you needed any more encouragement to make this—there is just one pan to wash!**

INGREDIENTS FOR THE FILLING:

2 tablespoons coconut oil

1 tablespoon coconut palm sugar

3 apples, cubed

½ teaspoon cinnamon

½ teaspoon allspice

¼ teaspoon ground ginger

1 cup blueberries

INGREDIENTS FOR THE BATTER:

¾ cup almond flour

¼ cup coconut milk

1 egg, beaten

3 tablespoons coconut sugar

1 tablespoon coconut oil, melted

1 teaspoon vanilla extract

½ teaspoon baking powder

Pinch of salt

DIRECTIONS:

1. Preheat the oven to 400°F.
2. Melt the coconut oil and sugar together in an oven-proof skillet over a high heat. Add the apples and spices, and cook until the apples are caramelized and brown—about 5 minutes.
3. Now make the batter by mixing all the ingredients together in a bowl.
4. Add the blueberries to the skillet and cook for a further 2 minutes, then pour the batter over everything.
5. Pop the whole skillet in the oven and allow it to bake for 20 minutes or until the cake is golden brown on the top and the batter is set through.
6. Remove the cake from the oven and allow it to cool down slightly, then slice and serve with a dollop of whipped coconut cream.

CHOCOLATE HEAVEN

Yields: 8 Servings

INGREDIENTS FOR THE BOTTOM LAYER:

1½ cups coconut palm sugar

1 cup coconut oil, plus more for greasing

¾ cup cocoa powder, unsweetened

½ cup coconut milk

½ cup almond butter

½ cup coconut flour

2 eggs

1 tablespoon apple cider vinegar

1 teaspoon vanilla extract

1 teaspoon baking soda

½ teaspoon baking powder

½ teaspoon salt

1 cup zucchini, grated (dried off with paper towels)

1 cup dark chocolate (70–90% cocoa), grated

INGREDIENTS FOR THE MIDDLE LAYER:

4 ripe avocados, peeled and pitted

8 dates, soaked in warm water for 10 minutes then pitted

1 cup cocoa powder, unsweetened

½ cup raw honey

¼ cup almond milk

1 tablespoon vanilla extract

¼ teaspoon cinnamon

¼ teaspoon salt

INGREDIENTS FOR THE TOP LAYER:

1 cup palm shortening

½ cup coconut milk

¼ cup almond milk

¼ cup coconut flour

¼ cup raw honey

2 tablespoons coconut oil, melted

1 tablespoon maple syrup

1 tablespoon arrowroot powder

1 tablespoon vanilla extract

¼ teaspoon cinnamon

¼ teaspoon salt

1 cup dark chocolate (70–90% cocoa), grated

DIRECTIONS:

The Bottom Layer

1. Preheat the oven to 350°F and grease a 9 x 13 oven-proof glass dish with coconut oil.
2. Add the ingredients to a large mixing bowl, leaving the zucchini and chocolate until last, and stir together well.
3. Pour the batter into your prepared dish and bake for 30 minutes or until a toothpick inserted in the middle comes out clean. Remove from the oven and cool.

The Middle Layer

1. Place everything into the blender and purée until smooth. Transfer to a bowl and chill in the fridge.

The Top Layer

1. Place all the ingredients except the grated chocolate into the blender and mix until well combined. The mixture should resemble whipped cream. Transfer the mixture into a bowl and place it into the fridge to chill.

To Assemble

1. Spread the middle layer on top of the cooled cake with a rubber spatula in an even layer, then spoon the whipped cream on top. Finish off with some grated dark chocolate sprinkled over the top.
2. Slice and serve!

BANANA SPLIT!

Yields: 2 Servings

> **A great dessert for sharing with a loved one!**

INGREDIENTS:

2 bananas, peeled

2 tablespoons nut butter (your favorite)

1 tablespoon pecan nuts, chopped

1 teaspoon cinnamon

DIRECTIONS:

1. Preheat the oven to 375° F.
2. Use a knife to slice the bananas lengthways, about a third of the way through, then use the back of a spoon to push the sides away from each other to make space for the nut butter.
3. Spoon the nut butter into the opening carefully—don't split the banana.
4. Sprinkle with cinnamon and nuts, then wrap them up with aluminum foil.
5. Bake for 15 minutes.
6. Remove from the oven and allow to cool until you are able to handle them comfortably.
7. Plate and serve.

PALEO-INSPIRED CINNA-ROLL

Yields: 1 Serving

INGREDIENTS:

2 tablespoons olive oil

2 tablespoons almond milk

2 tablespoons raw honey

1 egg

½ teaspoon cinnamon

¼ teaspoon vanilla extract

¼ teaspoon nutmeg

¼ teaspoon baking soda

Pinch of salt

4 tablespoons coconut flour (more if the batter is very thin)

½–1 cup chopped dried fruit of your choice

DIRECTIONS:

1. Preheat the oven to 375° F.
2. Combine everything except the dried fruit in a bowl and mix together well. Allow the batter to rest for 10 minutes.
3. Spoon the batter onto a parchment-lined baking tray and mold it into a ½-inch-thick rectangle.
4. Spread the chopped dried fruit out on top and add some more cinnamon.
5. Use the edge of the parchment paper to help you roll the rectangle up like a Swiss roll. The batter should be quite soft, so this can be difficult—go slowly and be patient.
6. Bake in the oven for 25 minutes or until the roll is golden brown.
7. Remove from the oven, allow to cool down slightly, then top with a dollop of whipped coconut cream and dig in!

CARAMEL CRUNCH BITES

Yields: 4—6 Servings

Perfect for sharing with friends!

INGREDIENTS:

½ cup coconut milk

½ cup coconut oil

1½ cups coconut palm sugar

1 tablespoon vanilla extract

½ cup almond butter

¼ teaspoon salt

2½ cups shredded coconut

1 cup coconut flakes

1 cup dark chocolate (70–90% cocoa), cut into chunks

DIRECTIONS:

1. Place the coconut milk, coconut oil, and coconut sugar into a saucepan, and bring to a boil over a medium heat. Allow to boil, stirring constantly for 5 minutes or until the caramel thickens.
2. Remove from the heat and stir in the vanilla, almond butter, and salt.
3. Now stir in the shredded coconut.
4. Finally, add the chocolate chunks. At this stage, don't stir too much, as you want to keep the chocolate as intact as possible.
5. Line a baking tray with parchment paper and portion out the dough in equal quantities (about a tablespoon or 2 per bite).
6. Allow to cool at room temperature for about 4 hours to allow them to set properly.

STRAWBERRY ICE CREAM WITH BUTTER CRUNCH

Yields: 2 Servings

INGREDIENTS FOR THE ICE CREAM:

1 can coconut milk

¼ cup raw honey

2 tablespoons vanilla extract

1 cup strawberries, quartered

INGREDIENTS FOR THE CRUNCH:

⅓ cup almond flour

¼ cup almond butter

2 tablespoons raw honey

1 teaspoon vanilla extract

Pinch of salt

DIRECTIONS:

The Ice Cream

1. Place coconut milk, raw honey, and vanilla into a saucepan and allow them to just heat through over a medium heat, stirring constantly. Transfer the mixture to a bowl and place it into the freezer for 2 hours.
2. Add the strawberries to a clean saucepan and bring to a gentle boil. Allow to continue cooking until the strawberries break down into a chunky sauce. Store in the fridge.

The Crunch

1. Combine all the ingredients together and mix until you get a crumbly texture. Refrigerate.
2. After 2 hours, move the mixture from the freezer into the ice-cream maker, along with the strawberries, and blend according to the manufacturer's directions.
3. When the ice cream is ready, divide it between 2 bowls and top with the butter crunch.

SMOOTHIES

CHOCOLATE DELIGHT

Yields: 1 Serving

INGREDIENTS:

1½ cups ice cubes

½ cup almond milk

¼ cup almond butter

1 large ripe banana

2 tablespoons raw cacao powder

DIRECTIONS:

1. Throw it all into the blender and blitz until smooth and creamy.
2. Tastes like a chocolate milkshake—awesome right?

PALEO PROTEIN POWER PUNCH

Yields: 1 Serving

Easy, on-the-go protein drink to fill you up!

INGREDIENTS:

1 cup almond milk

2 eggs

2 bananas

1 tablespoon raw honey

2 teaspoons vanilla extract

1 teaspoon cinnamon

DIRECTIONS:

1. Put it in the blender and blitz until smooth.
2. Gulp it down and heal!

GREEN MACHINE!

Yields: 1 Serving

INGREDIENTS:

1 cup ice

1 cup almond milk

1 cup kale, washed

1 ripe banana

½ teaspoon vanilla extract

¼ cup whipped coconut cream for garnish

½ teaspoon freshly chopped mint for garnish

DIRECTIONS:

1. Put everything into your blender and whip it until smooth.
2. Pour it into a glass and top with the whipped coconut cream.
3. Finish off with a sprinkle of freshly chopped mint.
4. Slide in a straw, sip, and feel your body revitalize.

CONCLUSION

The Paleo diet does not ask you to believe false promises. You do not have to starve yourself, nor kill yourself working out. There is no fasting, no detox, no fancy pills or potions, and no weighing every morsel that goes into your mouth. All that is required of you is to make a conscious decision to do what you can to be healthy. You only have to do what your body is naturally designed to do anyway—eat good food, exercise daily, and limit stress in your life. There are no limits—you eat until you are satisfied, and that means less chance of falling off the proverbial wagon.

Because you are "fixing" your body naturally from the inside, you can feel the effects very soon after embarking on this lifestyle, and therein lies the motivation to continue.

Will there be setbacks? Undoubtedly.

Is it the end of the world? Of course not!

Simply pick yourself up, dust yourself off, and continue on your Paleo journey. It's fun, it's educational, it's healthy, and above all else, it's totally delicious!

The Paleo diet is totally doable once you set your mind to it. You have got absolutely nothing to lose and everything to gain by giving it a try.

What are you waiting for?